TO FIND A JOB...
START A NEW CAREER

TO FIND A JOB...
START A NEW CAREER

The Career and Job Change Toolbox

MARVIN RAFAL, Ph.D.

**Andrews McMeel
Publishing**
Kansas City

03 04 05 06 07 MLT 10 9 8 7 6 5 4 3 2 1

Library of Congress Cataloging-in-Publication Data
Rafal, Marvin.
    To find a job—start a new career : the career- and job-change toolbox /
by Marvin Rafal.
    p. cm.
    ISBN 0-7407-3854-2
    1. Career changes. 2. Job hunting. I. Title.

HF5384.R34 2003
650.14—dc21   2003045238

CONTENTS

TO FIND A JOB...
START A NEW CAREER

INTRODUCTION

Millions of Americans aren't working ... but, thank God, they've got jobs!

—*Old joke*

IN HIS 1974 but still contemporary book *Working*, Studs Terkel quotes William Faulkner as saying, "You can't eat for eight hours a day, nor make love for eight hours a day. All you can do for eight hours a day is work. Which is the reason why man makes himself and everybody else so miserable and unhappy."

Perhaps that's why the Department of Labor estimates the median time an employee stays with the same employer is three and a half years. In the current workforce, it has become a rare occurrence for an employee to keep one job for a lifetime and retire there. Moreover, with today's high jobless rate, hundreds of thousands of people are looking for work at which, according to Faulkner, they may be miserable.

This book has been written to meet what may be a reader's immediate need: to succeed in getting the right job as quickly as possible. If you can identify with any of the following, this book is for you.

- You have recently become unemployed, because your company downsized or for other reasons. You hope your next job will provide not only stability but also satisfaction.

- You are still employed but sense that downsizing is about to happen. What can you do to be prepared for when the ax falls?

- Your job doesn't fit and you need to rethink your career. But you don't really know what your goals or your opportunities are. How do you find out?

- You want your boss's job, but it looks like he or she is going to be in it for quite a while. What are your options?

- You think another area of your company offers greater opportunities for growth. How can you be sure?

- You've been in your job for quite a while and feel you've mastered it. You want some new challenges. What might they be?

- You feel trapped by your own experience, success, and salary level. You're good at what you do and you're well paid. Your organization would not be unhappy if you keep doing what you do so well. You might want something new. How do you proceed?

- You're a person with high potential. Your problem is too many options. Which direction do you choose?

- You've achieved your career goals as you set them some years ago, but now you've changed. Has it been worthwhile?

- You know exactly what you want, but you can't get it. Maybe it's a transfer, maybe a promotion. You've talked to your boss and to the human resources department, but nothing has happened so far. What next?

- Significant changes have occurred in your life: children are born or leave home, you get married or divorced, your spouse gets or loses a job, your health improves or deteriorates. Can you adjust to these changes in your current job, or do you need to think of making a change?

- You're perfectly happy. You like your job. But the company and the industry are changing. Your job might be modified. Are you ready for this to happen?

Why Work Is So Important

If someone were to ask why you work, you would probably say that you need the money. You might add that ever since the Garden of Eden, human beings have had to work to earn food, shelter, and clothing.

But that answer is not the whole story. It doesn't explain why some people work as volunteers, for no money, just as diligently as others who get paid. Neither does it account for people who have a great deal of money, yet continue to work, or for those who work at jobs that do not pay very well, when they could qualify for employment that paid much better.

It is clear that work meets many needs other than money. Some people need to be creative, others to socialize, others to help people, still others to gain prestige and status. And despite occasional complaints (griping is part of our tradition), human beings derive considerable psychological satisfaction from their work.

Most people in the United States possess some choice concerning the work they do. In fact, the right to decide what we do, when, and for whom is one of our most highly prized freedoms, and though people do not always exercise this freedom, they value it highly.

Just as work can provide both financial rewards and psychological ones, however, it can also fail to meet these needs or, worse, can actually cause psychological distress. This book, therefore, has an overarching purpose: to help you find and choose work that meets as many of your needs, economic and psychological, as possible.

The Need for Job Satisfaction

By some estimates, 20 million people in the United States are dissatisfied with their jobs, even though they stay in them. And many of them incur substantial penalties as a result.

People unhappy with their jobs may actually experience physical problems in the form of headaches, loss of sleep, chronic fatigue, frequent respiratory infections, and loss of sleep. They also suffer emotional consequences: depression, irritability (both of which can lead to problems at home), worry, and a feeling of lessened self-worth. Nor are they spared such side effects as lack of motivation, boredom, inability to concentrate both on and off the job, and negativism.

It was therefore not surprising when a study reported by *Business Week* revealed that in the second quarter of 2001 about one in five people, or 20 percent of the workforce, made changes. The figures were are follows:

6   percent of the workforce changed employers voluntarily
4.5 percent stayed with their employers but changed jobs
3.2 percent retired
2.5 percent were laid off but found a new job
2.4 percent were laid off and are unemployed
1.1 percent became self-employed

To achieve job satisfaction, you must first make a realistic determination of your own capabilities and ambitions. You alone are responsible for your career planning. No one can do it for you. This realization may be the hardest basic task you have to face. It comes down to the question of what you want to accomplish in your life and the trade-offs you may need to make to achieve them.

The first step is to reflect on what kind of activities you do best. Over the long haul, how well you perform in a job, in most cases, ultimately leads to job success. Above-average performers advance further and faster than average performers. *How to Succeed in Business Without Really Trying* is a successful musical, but it is not a successful scenario in real life.

A danger that needs to be faced is choosing security over challenge, or present salary over a high-potential job with somewhat less pay initially, or present circumstances (including home and location) for a new environment that would require a new adjustment. If you fall into a rut you may become unable to make a change in future if it ever becomes necessary.

You will need to obtain up-to-date, accurate, and comprehensive information about what's out there in the way of job opportunities, industry trends, and the status and credentials of potential employers. You should secure information on the range of career choices available to you and the personal requirements for a variety of occupations.

Finally, bear in mind that career goals and choices can change with increases in your experience and maturity. Everyone goes through a sequence of stages, referred to as a life cycle, as they grow older. In an early stage, roughly from ages twenty-one to thirty-five, people acquire skills and the knowledge to use those skills. This is a time of great energy and creativity.

At roughly ages thirty-five to fifty-five, people have developed their abilities, have acquired a reputation for their competence, and are closely connected to their profession or company or organization. This is a mature stage in the life cycle.

Then, above the age of fifty-five, people usually begin gradually to lessen their attachment to their profession or organization, even though they are still contributing. They begin to think about retirement and even to review their histories, how they have lived and what they have accomplished.

It is clear that as these changes occur so do career choices, goals, and objectives change. (A more complete description of life and career changes is given in Chapter 7.)

Technological change usually carries with it the need for new skills and new careers. Retraining, needed for adjusting to these new technologies, can even become a continuous process.

How This Book Is Organized:

Part I: Rethinking Your Job

This section deals with assessing a present or prospective job, so as to compare what you want from a job with what you are receiving. The inventories that are included enable you to establish whether your needs are being met and, if shortcomings exist, what they are.

Part II: Rethinking Your Career

This section helps analyze whether you are on the path to a career that works for you. It asks what "season" you are in, what stage in your life, and where you stand among the factors that contribute to your job satisfaction.

Part III: Learning Self-Assessment

The exercises provided in this section will help you secure answers to the question "Who am I?" By evaluating your values, interests, personality, and job preferences, you are taking the first steps in identifying jobs that will be a good fit.

Part IV: Identifying Appropriate Jobs

What's the match with who I am? The text and tailor-made charts show you how to compare your job preferences with the requirements of different available jobs and how to start career planning to set up and achieve your long-term vocational goals.

Part V: Getting to Where You Want to Be

Now you are ready to decide where you stand and where you need to go in your career. Is your present job right for you? Is it right with some modifications? Completely wrong?

Part VI: Finding a Job That Fits

This section begins with what to do when you suspect the ax is about to fall, directs you in coping with the steps in the hiring process, and ends with getting the job. Because more and more people in or near retirement have begun thinking about continuing or returning to work, the last chapter deals specifically with older workers who, by choice or necessity, wish to restart a career.

The Management Point of View

Finally, a word about point of view, especially in those chapters that deal with finding and getting a job. My career has involved helping business management to recruit candidates for employment, select those likely to fit, stay, and grow, and further evaluate those individuals who have the potential to advance to management positions. My intention, therefore, is to describe to the job seeker, or the person rethinking his or her career, what management looks for, how management judges what it sees, and how it evaluates its employees for raises, bonuses, and promotions.

PART I

Rethinking Your Job

Legendary football coach John Heisman, for whom the Heisman trophy was named, explained on the first day of practice that a football was " . . . a prolate spheroid—that is, an elongated sphere—in which the outer leather casing is drawn tightly over a somewhat smaller rubber tubing. . . . Better to have died a small boy than to fumble this."

What should one say about fumbling a career?

CHAPTER **1**

The First Step

THE FIRST STEP is to evaluate the various factors in a given job that make it more or less suitable for you. These factors have been grouped under three headings: (1) the organization, (2) the environment of the job, and (3) the work itself. Under each heading you will find a list of factors, along with a description where appropriate. An inventory follows that gives you an opportunity to rate each factor according to the degree of satisfaction or dissatisfaction it affords you.

The Organization

If you want or need more information about your company, you can obtain it from a variety of sources. If your company is a public one, it publishes an annual report for its stockholders. Sometimes you can find articles in newspapers and magazines.

Directories provide details, particularly about larger companies, as to their size, earnings, number of employees, location of plants and offices, and other facts of importance. Important directories include:

Thomas' Register of American Manufacturers
Moody's Industrial Manual
Standard and Poor's Register of Corporations
Dun and Bradstreet's Million Dollar Directory
Ward's Business Directory

Is It a Good Fit?

Consider the degree of fit between you and your organization's history, financial status, products or services, activities, philosophy, ethics, and goals by asking yourself these questions:

- Are your company's policies and methods clear, understandable, and practical?

- When your company does its planning, does it consult its employees?

- Are your company's goals consistent with the methods used to accomplish them?

- Is the company's leadership effective and well respected and does it inspire the rest of the organization to do good work?

- To what degree is the atmosphere of the entire organization healthy because the overall philosophy of the company is healthy?

What Are the Industry Prospects?

Companies that are part of a growing industry are more likely to be successful and prosperous. Every two years, the Bureau of Labor Statistics of the U.S. Department of Labor publishes long-term projections of output and employment for more than 200 industries. This covers the entire U.S. economy.

The *U.S. Industry and Trade Outlook*, an annual publication of the U.S. Department of Commerce, lists growth potential for a number of industries and their globalization.

What Are the Promotion Possibilities?

Ask yourself these questions:

- Does your organization allow you to apply for appropriate jobs in other sections or departments of the company as well as in your own?

- Do you have to compete with outside applicants when advancement opportunities arise?

- How long is it likely to be before the next step up your career ladder becomes available?

- Does your company provide you with opportunities through training programs to qualify for positions of greater authority or responsibility?

- Do you see yourself with a future in this company?

How Good Is Job Security?

Ask yourself these questions:

- Have you noted high turnover among your fellow employees?

- Is this turnover related to dissatisfaction—either with the company, the working conditions, or the work itself?

Is the Size of the Organization Right for You?

Size is associated with unique characteristics. Smaller companies tend to allow closer association with executives. Their employees may have wider responsibilities and more varied job duties.

Larger companies have more supervisory and managerial openings. They may provide better employee benefits and may offer more ambitious training programs. But their jobs may be more specialized, with a more limited variety of job duties and responsibilities.

Is the Company New or Well Established?

Long-established companies are less likely to fail and may have the reputation of being among the leaders in their industry. But they may be slower to react to changes in the marketplace or to technological advances.

Younger companies may offer a more exciting and challenging environment and, if successful, share their success with their employees. But the failure rate among new firms is high.

Is the Company Privately or Publicly Owned?

Privately owned companies often make efforts to treat their employees as part of a family and may sometimes be in a position to stretch the rules to cover an employee's special needs. But higher-level jobs may be reserved for members of the owning family.

Public companies are more likely to promote employees to higher-level jobs on the basis of merit but are also likely to treat their employees more impersonally.

The Environment of the Job

Often, even when the company and the work itself are acceptable, the conditions—the surroundings of the job—are not. Here are some of the more important factors for you to evaluate.

How Good Are Compensation and Benefits?

You'll need a benchmark to evaluate the typical compensation and benefits package for your kind of job. You can gather some information by studying want ads in the newspapers for comparable jobs. Networking among friends, relatives, and acquaintances may uncover additional information.

Be sure to check your company's policy about overtime pay. Also include the benefits package in your evaluation, whether you have to contribute to it and, if so, how much.

One warning: Take the location of your job into consideration. Costs of living are generally higher—sometimes substantially so—in large metropolitan areas than in smaller cities, rural areas, and some suburbs.

Important sources of national, state, and metropolitan-area data are available from the National Compensation Survey. This combines figures from three Bureau of Labor Statistics programs: the Employment Cost Index, the Occupational Compensation Survey, and the Employee Benefits Survey. You can obtain these data from:

Bureau of Labor Statistics Office of Compensation and
    Working Conditions
2 Massachusetts Avenue, NE, Room 4130
Washington, DC 20212-0001
(202) 691-6199
Internet: http://stats.bls.gov/ncs

Now ask yourself: Is the pay appropriate for the work you do?

Are the Hours Satisfactory?

The conventional hours of employment for most jobs are eight hours a day, five days a week, for a total of forty hours, but there are variations. In some companies, overtime is a major factor, for seasonal or other reasons. Weekend, holiday, and night work are other variations.

Consider: Do the hours adversely affect your school or family commitments?

Is the Location of the Job OK?

One consideration, of course, is commuting—its expense and time. And there are others: the cost of housing, the cost of living in the area in general, recreational resources, educational institutions and their availability, and climate.

Do You Get Along with Coworkers?

Ask yourself these questions:

- Are you finding that groups have been formed to protect their own interests?

- Have cliques developed, and do they operate to control the activities of their members?

- Do you prefer not to mix with your coworkers on and off the job, or do you associate actively with them?

What Are Your Relations with the Boss?

Ask yourself these questions:

- Do your supervisors help you to improve your skills and support your efforts toward advancement?

- Do they get along with you and your coworkers for reasons other than just to maintain good relations and avoid friction?

- Are communications with your supervisors and with other key people easy?

- Do your supervisors support your work activities and efforts?

- Do your supervisors allow you to become involved in decisions that have to do with your work?

- Do your supervisors give you feedback about your work, good or bad?

- Are your supervisors friendly toward you?

- Do you respect your immediate supervisor's abilities?

- If you had a choice, would you select someone else as your immediate supervisor?

- Do you find it hard to do your work because you have difficulty reaching your supervisor for consultations?

The Work Itself

It is almost an axiom that people do their best work when they enjoy what they are doing. What we have evaluated to this point are the organization and the surroundings of the job. Now we need to evaluate the work itself.

What really matters is whether the nature of the work suits your interests, values, personality, and the other factors that make up who you are. Parts III and IV provide specific directions for analyzing what kind of work is a good fit. For now, answering the questions that follow may help you evaluate whether the work you are doing provides the satisfactions that enable you to say you like your work.

Is Your Work Important and Challenging?

To decide if your work involves clear-cut challenging responsibilities that are important to the company, ask yourself these questions:

- Can you see that the work you do fits into the organization's goals and mission?

- Are you consulted when management is thinking about changes in the area of work that is your responsibility?

- Do you have sufficient opportunities to make independent decisions about your work?

- Do you have a sufficient amount of control in that part of your work that is your personal responsibility?

- Do the quantity and/or quality of your work affect the work of others?

- Are you allowed to take personal accountability for the outcome of your work?

- How frequently does management make decisions about your work without consulting you or asking your advice?

Are Your Achievements Clearly Visible?

Your work should permit you to have obvious accomplishments from time to time. Ask yourself these questions:

- To what degree do the tasks of your job bring you satisfaction?

- Are you responsible for the completion of a specific piece of work?

- To what degree do you find yourself motivated on the job?

- How much satisfaction do you gain from performing your duties and activities?

- To what degree are you able to recognize that you are performing well on this job? (The answer to the last question is based on the fact that while you are pleased if your supervisors and coworkers recognize your good performance, the really important thing is that *you* recognize it.)

Do Your Responsibilities Increase as Your Skills Improve?

As you continue to perform well, you should see a gradual increase in your skills. If so, your job assignments should gain in importance, with an increased eligibility for advancement. Ask yourself these questions:

- To what degree does the job require you to use a variety of skills and talents to deal with a variety of tasks?

- To what degree is your future in this position limited or unlimited?

- Aside from the matter of advancement, to what degree do you have opportunities for personal growth and development?

How appropriate is your workload?

Ask yourself these questions:

- Are you able to handle your assigned work effectively within an expected time frame?

- Do you feel the quantity of output expected from you is fair and proper?

Is your work interesting and varied?

Ask yourself these questions:

- To what degree do your tasks and activities continue to bring you job satisfaction?

- Do you have sufficient opportunities to learn new things?

CHAPTER 2

Evaluating Job Satisfaction Using the Inventory

THIS INVENTORY will help you in evaluating your job and your satisfaction with it. It is valuable both in evaluating a job offer and in considering future job possibilities. The inventory uses the same three headings found in Chapter 1: the organization, the environment of the job, and the work itself.

A scale representing your degree of satisfaction or dissatisfaction with your present job, from 1 (low) to 5 (high), is provided in the five columns to the right. Rate yourself by placing a check in the appropriate column.

The Organization

Level of Satisfaction	LOW 1	2	3	4	HIGH 5
Your company's philosophy, history, financial status, business, activities, and goals	☐	☐	☐	☐	☐
The prospects for the industry in which your company is represented	☐	☐	☐	☐	☐
Your promotion possibilities in your company	☐	☐	☐	☐	☐
Job security for you within your company	☐	☐	☐	☐	☐
The size of the company vs. your needs and wants	☐	☐	☐	☐	☐
The degree to which whether the company is new or established influences you	☐	☐	☐	☐	☐
The degree to which whether the company is publicly or privately owned influences you	☐	☐	☐	☐	☐

The Environment of the Job

Level of Satisfaction	LOW 1	2	3	4	HIGH 5
The degree to which you are satisfied with the compensation and benefits offered by your company	☐	☐	☐	☐	☐
The extent to which you find the hours of employment and the required overtime to be acceptable	☐	☐	☐	☐	☐
Your satisfaction with the area In which you live, including cost of living	☐	☐	☐	☐	☐
The degree to which your relationships with coworkers enable you to function appropriately	☐	☐	☐	☐	☐
Your rating of your relationships with your supervisors	☐	☐	☐	☐	☐
Your assessment of the working conditions (consider such factors as space, lighting, heating, and cooling)	☐	☐	☐	☐	☐

The Work Itself

Level of Satisfaction	LOW 1	2	3	4	HIGH 5
The extent to which the work involves clear-cut challenging responsibilities that are important to the company	□	□	□	□	□
The extent to which you are you able to succeed in achieving desired results—accomplishments that are not only obvious to others but to you as well	□	□	□	□	□
The degree to which you notice improvement in your skills, increasing importance in your job assignments, as well as increased eligibility for advancement	□	□	□	□	□
The extent to which you consider your workload to be satisfactory	□	□	□	□	□
The extent to which you feel you receive adequate recognition for doing the job well	□	□	□	□	□

Summary

Completing this three-part inventory gives you an opportunity to evaluate your job with some degree of system and organization. In addition, you are in a position to identify those elements that are contributing the most to your satisfaction or dissatisfaction.

Your evaluation is, of course, subjective. It is based on your personal judgments, values, interests, and preferences. Within your company, perhaps even in your department or work team, one person may see the company and the work as excellent, while another person may have an entirely different view.

All these judgments are legitimate, based on individual preferences. How each person perceives his or her job is reality for that person, and the analysis provided by the inventory gives you an opportunity to think about your vocational situation without making snap judgments.

The following suggestions can introduce further discipline to your evaluation:

- Conduct your analysis from the long-term perspective of your career goals.

- If you need to put a more positive spin on your analysis, consider whether you can make favorable changes within your present position.

- Ask yourself, Which factors are within my control? Over which factors do I have little or no control?

- Keep in mind that times change and situations change, sometimes for the better, sometimes not.

Basically, you have three options: (1) change (behaviors, goals, or circumstances); (2) stay (if this decision is the one that best suits your needs); or (3) leave (to find another outlet for your energies, abilities, and potentials).

Finally, your analysis needs to take into account more than just your present job. Consider the following four factors:

The Industry

- Who are the leaders—the companies, individuals, and even nations?

- What new technologies have affected your company in recent years, and what is the company doing to deal with them?

- Have you networked to keep abreast of these changes?

- Are you aware of them through newspaper articles, trade papers, advertising campaigns, and annual statements?

The Company

- Do you read between the lines of your company's publications and news releases?

- Have the technological changes of recent years had an impact on labor costs, products, or services?

- Has the company formed alliances or mergers or moved into global markets?

- Do or will these changes require a new set of skills on your part, and new goals and career choices?

Your Specialization or Expertise

If you are relatively young, you may be busy exploring different opportunities and areas of specialization and expertise. If so, keep in mind how these areas are changing and what the likely future is for them. If you consider yourself an expert or master of some discipline, ask yourself if, in your concentration on your job, you have allowed yourself to become obsolete because that discipline is changing. Ask yourself:

- Has this job and the work involved changed in the past few years, so that different skills are required?

- Are changes likely to take place in the near future?

- What new and different skills, abilities, or knowledge will you need to be successful?

- Can you contribute ideas to the company to help it adjust to changes?

Your Personal Needs

Your circumstances are constantly changing, and the changes are likely to affect your vocational decisions. You should choose jobs or companies that meet your personal needs and at the same time provide opportunities for reward, challenge, enhanced skills and learning, and support. Ask yourself:

- Do you need to cut down on your travel or commuting time?

- Is job security becoming more important than job growth?

- Are you newly married or contemplating marriage, and does your spouse (or spouse to be) also have career goals?

- Do your children have special health or educational needs?

- Do you want to be able to spend more time on your hobbies or avocations?

- Do you need to move to some other part of the country?

- Are you facing divorce?

- Are responsibilities toward parents likely to impact on your work situation?

Evaluating Your Job Satisfaction

This book's introduction makes the point that even though people occasionally complain, they often actually derive considerable satisfaction from their work. Hence, complaints about work and about job dissatisfaction have to be evaluated and analyzed.

Ask yourself if your dissatisfaction is realistic. Certain experiences you encounter in your job are inevitable and probably always will be in this less-than-perfect world. It is not uncommon to fail to get the credit you deserve for some job accomplishment. Sometimes unreasonable deadlines are set, for example. Or bosses may not pay attention to the ideas and suggestions you submit.

Many of these experiences can be encountered in almost any job, and there is probably not much you can do about them. But it is doubtful if ordinary, garden-variety situations should, by themselves, lead you seriously to consider leaving. So it is important to determine whether your job dissatisfaction is so severe that you would be well advised to give notice. This introduces, in turn, the question of how to evaluate future employment so as to reduce the chances that you will again encounter the consequences of a job that is, for you, a bad fit.

In short, you need to evaluate whether your dissatisfaction is realistic—whether it is based on a fundamental incompatibility or on less important dissatisfactions that you can adjust to or, at least, learn to tolerate.

Downsizing

A frequent cause of job unhappiness occurs when a company downsizes, and the unhappiness can be almost as acute in people whose jobs are spared as in people who are separated. Even if you dodged the ax you may feel its effects.

People whose jobs are downsized may experience the following:

- They may be offered early retirement incentives.

- They may be offered incentives for voluntary separation.

- They may experience involuntary layoff.

Even when the separation package is financially generous, there may be a perception that one's sense of self-worth has been dealt a blow.

Those whose jobs have been spared may experience "survivor sickness," feelings of fear and anger. Sometimes, at the beginning of a period of downsizing, a company's employees may welcome the process because they may feel the company was bloated and non-competitive. Whether they continue to have these feelings or develop "survivor sickness" may depend largely on whether they believe the downsizing was handled wisely, based on objective analysis of the company's needs, or badly, and based on politics. If downsizing was handled badly, the survivors are likely to have many questions.

- Is the downsizing over, or will I have to sweat out wondering whether I will be among the next group to go?

- Has my old role changed, and, if so, what is my new role?

- How can I do my job efficiently when the old network on which I relied for getting the work done is destroyed or disrupted?

- Do I dare go out on a limb and do more than just the job's requirements, as I was encouraged to do and which made the job fun and challenging, or should I exercise greater caution and take few or no risks?

- Am I willing to continue to work in an environment where there is higher stress and lower morale, one where my associates show decreased motivation and pay less attention to the work itself?

- There is some evidence that, over time and in some situations, the environment improves and the deterioration in morale may not be permanent. Is it worth waiting in the expectation and hope that this will be the case in my company?

Prioritizing Your Job Wants

On the left side of an 8½-by-11 sheet of paper, prepare two columnar headings: WHAT I WANT IN A JOB and PRIORITY.

You should list eight or ten items in your WANT column. Next to each item, in the PRIORITY column, you should indicate its importance to you, with 1 as the most important, 2 as the next, 3 after that, and so on, until you have ranked each item in the order of its importance to you.

Your list may look something like this—with, of course, your own items and their priorities.

WHAT I WANT IN A JOB	PRIORITY
Job security	3
Decent income	1
Fair supervision	5
Capable associates	8
Opportunity to advance	2
Challenging work	4
Opportunity to achieve	7
Good working conditions	6
Information on company activity	9

Now add a new column immediately to the right of the first two. Head this third column PRESENT SITUATION.

Reevaluate the items from the standpoint of how you see the opportunity in your present job for meeting each of your needs.

Again, use 1 as representing the best opportunity, 2 as next best, and so on. If you are not presently employed, use your last job, or your past most important one, in your appraisal.

Your list may now look something like this:

WHAT I WANT IN A JOB	PRIORITY	PRESENT SITUATION
Job security	3	8
Decent income	1	2
Fair supervision	5	5
Capable associates	8	1
Opportunity to advance	2	7
Challenging work	4	3
Opportunity to achieve	7	4
Good working conditions	6	6
Information on company activity	9	9

Your analysis of the contrast between the importance to you of the factors you want in a job and what you seem to be securing should give you insights into the degree of your job's shortcomings and whether your needs are being met adequately.

Before you leave this analysis, consider that a company has its own needs, the most important of which is to be successful and profitable. The best scenario would be to achieve an interdependent relationship between your own needs and those of the company.

In subsequent chapters, you will have opportunities to explore how likely it is that this relationship can be achieved.

CHAPTER 3

Assessing Your Performance
the Way the Boss Does

The ant, a prodigy of strength,
Lifts objects twice his weight and length
And never stops or sighs or glowers
Because it's after working hours.
The ant has but one flaw I see:
To wit, he doesn't work for me.

—*Richard Armour*

YOU HAVE HAD an opportunity to evaluate your job (present or past) and, no doubt, your boss. In the real world, the opposite also takes place: Bosses observe and rate their employees. From these evaluations come promotions, raises, bonuses, demotions, and terminations.

The evaluations described here are based on individual assessments, not mass layoffs (often called downsizing) as during substantial downturns in the economy.

Bosses (managers, supervisors, business owners) watch their employees quite closely and evaluate their performance on the job. Where it is possible to do so, they carefully take into account the results the employee is supposed to achieve.

In a particular job, results can sometimes be measured, sometimes not. Nonetheless, either way, bosses also concern themselves with the behaviors and actions employees demonstrate on the job. For example, they are troubled by employees who produce results but upset the workforce by their abrasiveness. When results cannot be measured, the employees' actions and behaviors are all a boss can go by.

Many larger companies, through research, have identified those behaviors associated with successful job performance. They compare their employees' actions with these behaviors as part of their regular performance rating system. Even smaller companies, which may not have a formal performance rating system, are likely to take successful behaviors into account when they decide on raises, promotions, and other administrative action. Therefore, it would seem to be a good idea for a job holder or job seeker to learn what those successful behaviors are and then work on developing and using them.

The British military writes officer-fitness reports similar to a company's performance evaluation. The following are actual excerpts from these reports.

- His men would follow him anywhere, but only out of curiosity.

- This officer is really not so much of a has-been as a definitely-won't-be.

- When she opens her mouth, it seems that this is only to change whatever foot was previously in there.

- Since my last report, he has reached rock bottom and has started to dig.

- He sets low personal standards and then consistently fails to achieve them.

- He has the wisdom of youth and the energy of old age.

- This officer should go far, and the sooner she starts, the better.

- This man is depriving a village somewhere of an idiot.

These comments are funny, but they do not indicate why the bosses (in this case, the superior officers) made the statements they did or what behaviors they noted as the reason for their negative assessments.

One of the best ways to gain insights into the boss's point of view is to put yourself into his or her shoes.

Think about a coworker, past or present, whom you know well and whose job performance you have been or are presently able to observe. Pretend you are his or her manager or supervisor and that you are required to complete a performance rating.

The Ability to Interact Successfully

One of the important abilities this person needs to have has been identified as the ability to get along with coworkers and others even when the going is tough. This ability may be formally described by your company as the ability to interact successfully with other people in different situations and be persuasive despite pressures and stress.

The behaviors associated with this ability have also been identified on a scale ranging from EXCELLENT to ABOVE AVERAGE, AVERAGE, BELOW AVERAGE and, finally, to NEEDS IMPROVEMENT.

Your job is to put a check mark to the left of any behaviors you think are typical of this person's performance for each of these five categories. Once you have completed your assessment, notice in which of the categories, from EXCELLENT down, most of the check marks have clustered. That would be your rating as the manager of this person.

Excellent

☐ Reacts positively, thoughtfully, and calmly to other people and situations regardless of pressure or stress. Looks for solutions to problems creating stress rather than trying to place blame.

☐ Responds to situations in an adult, problem-solving manner, referring to past successes and experiences to gain positive response from others.

☐ When faced with stress situations, always presents acceptable alternatives that will reach original goals yet maintain cooperation.

☐ Relates effectively to a wide variety of people in different departments to elicit needed assistance. Displays ability to relate well to persons with widely different personality types and management styles.

☐ Anticipates the feelings and responses of others, acknowledges and accepts their right to hold such feelings, and deals with them accurately.

Above Average

☐ Works well with authority figures; implements the policies of others smoothly.

☐ Remains objective and pursues relevant facts regardless of the stress or pressure applied by other individuals.

☐ Accurately identifies people's strengths and weaknesses. Utilizes their strengths and tries to shore up their weaknesses.

☐ Successfully presents persuasive dialogue regardless of stress applied by other individuals.

☐ Prioritizes multiple projects and relates this to involved personnel.

☐ Displays a positive, thoughtful, solution-seeking, objective, and diplomatic approach when working with people.

☐ Collaborates with others to define problem areas.

☐ Helps others analyze problems.

☐ Picks up feelings better than most, including subtle clues; anticipates responses.

Average

☐ Acts in a cooperative and participative manner. Acts independently when required to do so even when not entirely comfortable.

☐ Successfully conceals hostile feelings to avoid social conflict, when roots of conflict cannot be resolved.

☐ Usually works well with authority people and policy but on occasion shows defensiveness in response to criticism or rivalry.

☐ Responds in a logical and adequate manner but projects minimal warmth by using a mechanical approach.

☐ Shows interest in the other person.

☐ Helps the other person to generate solutions.

☐ Contributes suggestions from experience and knowledge.

Below Average

☐ Picks up feelings and body language, but glibly, which may result in his or her underestimating importance or depth of feelings; hence, may try to manipulate.

☐ Denies any need for others and insists on standing alone.

☐ Responds in an unpredictable manner, sometimes displaying easy relationship, sometimes showing feelings of discomfort.

☐ Does not show flexibility in relating to others; stresses own agenda and getting own way.

☐ Overreacts in critical decision-making situations.

☐ When required to sell an idea in difficult circumstances, gives up too quickly (or persists too long).

☐ Communicates poorly with problem person; withdraws from situation or is overaggressive in dealing with the person.

☐ Focuses only on own personal success and rewards.

Needs Improvement

☐ Aggressively maintains own position in spite of other people's recommendations and facts.

☐ Overreacts, responding before thoroughly discussing and analyzing the situation.

☐ Does nothing to solve the problems, perhaps hoping that the situation will subside without actions.

☐ Always challenges bosses and questions home office policy.

☐ Assumes position of armed truce with authority people and policies. Expresses hostility under guise of honesty and tries to manipulate boss.

☐ Loses temper when faced with a difficult interpersonal situation.

☐ Creates hostility or defensiveness by becoming personally involved. Displays undue sensitivity and personal prejudices.

The Ability to Create and Follow a Timetable

Here is another important ability, as identified by your company, that deals with organization and the use of time: the ability to establish a timetable to plan for the execution of necessary activities and then implement this timetable.

Excellent

☐ Establishes critical path that leads to the earliest possible completion dates.

☐ Continually monitors results following effective implementation of plans and takes immediate corrective action if it becomes apparent that timetable is not being met.

☐ As business conditions change, does not continue with business-as-usual approach but, rather, takes change into account and responds accordingly.

Above Average

☐ Develops a realistic critical path, listing activities to be carried out and completed, with dates assigned for beginning and completing each activity.

☐ Sets up priorities in terms of a well-defined long-range approach.

☐ Keeps looking for ways around obstacles to timetable.

☐ Displays optimism and confidence that an effective solution will be found.

☐ Employs large variety of responses in order to resolve frustrations and employs different strategies relative to the situation in order to accomplish timetable.

☐ Sustains interest in face of discouragement but can begin to display some loss of zest and optimism.

☐ Modifies direction or strategy used in reaching goals on time as situations change.

☐ After making and implementing decision, watches for signs that the decision was wise or unwise and acts accordingly.

Average

☐ Demonstrates use of priority approach on a daily basis.

☐ Coordinates all the various department functions to achieve cohesiveness for implementation of the market plan.

☐ Obtains commitments from people whose actions are necessary if proper execution of the plan is to occur.

☐ Adequately adjusts or copes when faced with barriers.

Below Average

☐ Overlooks prioritizing multiple activities.

☐ Does not develop implementation assignments to ensure that timetable commitments are obtained.

☐ Develops a timetable without regard to other people's ability to act within the established time period.

☐ Crowds too many activities into short period.

☐ Fails to apportion specific time for planning and organization, including allowance for emergencies.

Needs Improvement

☐ Fails to organize or demonstrates poor organizational ability so that emergencies constantly arise.

☐ Shows lack of concern when timetable is not being met, suggesting loss of interest.

☐ Makes little effort to move things forward after encountering resistance or frustration to timetable or its implementation.

You have now completed a portion of an employee performance rating, just as a manager would have done.

Now comes the tough part: Rate yourself, using the same two abilities, with their behaviors. You may want to use a different-color pen or pencil, so as to differentiate this second assessment from the first one.

Keep in mind that being objective about yourself is not easy. Just do the best you can and then consider how this exercise can be valuable to you.

Employee Classification

Performance appraisals serve managers in several ways. One of their uses is to classify employees as an indication of future possible development or training or for such personnel action as transfers to a different department. Continued inadequate ratings can lead to dismissal.

The Unsuited

At the level closest to termination are those people seen as entirely unsuited for their jobs, for whatever reason, who do not produce and are not believed to be able to do so. It has been estimated that, at any given time, they constitute not more than 5 percent of the organization.

The Comers

At the opposite extreme, and perhaps in equal number, are those people regarded at any one time as comers—people high in productivity and believed to be capable of advancement and continued growth.

Both the Unsuited and the Comers are generally easily identified.

The Average Performers

The largest group consists of those employees who are quite satisfactory in their performance and productivity but who are believed to have little or no potential for advancement. These are the people who keep the department or the organization functioning day to day.

The Problem Children

Finally, and most puzzling to their bosses, are those whose levels of productivity are barely acceptable but who are seen as capable of doing a lot better. To management, they are the problem children, whose bosses are not quite sure as to what administrative action to take and, if economic conditions permit, may spend a lot of time soul-searching.

Bosses, too, are capable of indecisiveness, and some are "problem children" themselves. Furthermore, it is unpleasant to face an employee with a negative evaluation and even more unpleasant to face the employee with the decision to terminate.

As a result, the boss often spends a good deal of time in further training, counseling, and discussions in an attempt to motivate the person, usually without success. The delay is of no benefit to either the individual or the organization.

A better solution would be to identify a position for which the employee is better suited and in which he or she could make a useful contribution. But these successful moves are uncommon. Sometimes no such job exists in the organization, and sometimes the process of identifying which job fits which employee is imperfect.

The result is that many an employee remains mired in a job with no future and with the apprehension that sooner or later the ax will fall.

Implications for the Employee

What are the implications for the employee, in these circumstances that exist in too many organizations? How should employees who feel threatened with termination or demotion deal with the situation?

The Managers' Criteria

Insightful and disciplined managers and supervisors use the following criteria to evaluate whether their problem children should be terminated:

1. Just how bad is the performance of this employee?
2. Are applicants available for the position who have the skills and experience to succeed?
3. What is the impact on the department or company's other employees by the continued presence of a problem child? What happens to the motivation of productive employees when nonproductive employees are treated equally, and what happens to the respect they feel for management?
4. How much time, money, and effort would it take for the person to function at an acceptable level?

The Employee's Reaction

How should an employee who feels threatened with termination or demotion deal with the situation? There are five possible ways in which these problem children may choose to react.

1. One obvious response is that such employees give serious consideration to biting the bullet—resigning and starting anew with due consideration to finding a position with the right fit.
2. They should recognize that commitment to the company, loyalty, and dedication will, by themselves, carry an employee only so far.
3. They should be aware that if hardworking efforts do not result in an acceptable level of productivity, it is unlikely that they will be able to establish a stable, harmonious relationship with their employer.
4. They may also consider facing their supervisor or manager with their status, as the boss sees it. This could include clear-cut definitions of their roles and responsibilities. They could explore the support the boss is ready to give. They could ask for explicit standards of performance that reflect what the boss expects if their performance is to be rated satisfactory.
5. Assuming the boss is honest in responding to these questions, or sufficiently forthright to initiate them, employees should be ready to listen, aware that it is no easy task for the boss to provide feedback. Feelings of defensiveness at such a time are natural, but by being aware of the futility of arguing, such feelings can be managed.

The ability to judge one's own worth, to know how we affect others, and to improve our behaviors and relationships with others, are described in Part III as being among the factors most influential in job success or failure. This ability is likely to forestall the crisis of termination to begin with. Before the crisis arrives, an employee can explore which of the options to pursue. Should he or she stay with the job and take steps to bring about improvement and growth? Or would it be wiser to cut the cord and seek a better fit in a new job?

PART II

Rethinking Your Career

"Would you tell me, please, which way I ought to go from here?"
"That depends a good deal on where you want to get to," said
the cat.
"I don't much care where—" said Alice.
"Then it doesn't matter which way you go," said the cat.

—*Lewis Carroll*

CHAPTER **4**

The Importance of Career Planning

I have studied the enemy all my life. I have read the memoirs of his generals and his leaders. I have even read his philosophies and listened to his music. I have studied, in detail, the account of every damned one of his battles. I know exactly how he will react under any given set of circumstances and he hasn't the slightest idea of what I'm going to do. So when the time comes, I'm going to whip the hell out of him.

—*George S. Patton*

CAREER PLANNING IS a continual process of recognizing our career needs, strengths, and potential contributions, discovering the needs and opportunities in companies and other organizations, deciding what and how we need to learn, and achieving our lifestyles and goals in the most appropriate way. If you *don't* know where you're going, you'll probably wind up in the wrong place.

World War II General George S. Patton, a career soldier, set his goal early on and pursued it with singleness of purpose. On the other hand, consider this poem by the young Abraham Lincoln, "The Bear Hunt":

When first my father settled here,
'Twas then the frontier line:
The panther's screams filled night with fear
And bears preyed on the swine.

Fortunately, young Abe gave up poetry and became our sixteenth president.

In trying to manage our careers, we run the risk of neglecting or finding it difficult to:

- Meet both the requirements of our employer and our own personal needs

- Utilize many of our talents and skills in our jobs

- Change our career plans as circumstances change

- Keep pace and deal with new situations caused by economic, technological, and organizational changes

- Prepare for the unexpected

Without the ability to manage our careers, we are apt to make decisions that are neither in our own best interests nor in the best interests of the company. Career planning is needed to establish the fit between one's values, needs, and skills and the needs of the organization.

After careful career planning, you will:

- Understand organizational realities and view your role in terms of how you can best contribute to the achievement of your own success and that of the organization.

- Add to your ultimate or long-term career goals. This enables you to plan realistically for the next step—perhaps the development of greater proficiency, satisfaction, or contribution in your current position and the mastery of new skills in preparation for another position.

- Obtain relevant information that will help you to reinforce, modify, or abandon an objective or course of action. This includes information about the plans, needs, and functions of your present organization or one you may have an interest in joining, as well as information about your own performance-related strengths and weaknesses, values, goals, and assumptions.

- Identify on-the-job development opportunities, supplemented by off-the-job training and educational experiences.

- Discover ways by which you can improve your current position as well as identify positions to which you might move as part of your career development.

Career planning is a process; career development is the result of implementing your career plans. The success of your career planning can be measured by external criteria, such as title, compensation, and status in the organization, or by internal criteria, such as feelings of satisfaction, achievement, self-esteem, and personal growth.

Personal growth is viewed here as progress measured against specific goals. This progress does not necessarily mean a job change or a promotion; it may well result in increased satisfaction or better performance in your current job. The success of your career planning program can be measured by your satisfaction, growth, and productivity.

Consider the words of a brilliant student of human nature and a remarkable pitcher, Satchel Paige, writing fifty years ago on how to stay young. All people engaged in career planning or in rethinking their careers should follow his timeless advice.

Avoid fried meats, which angry up the blood. If your stomach disputes you, lie down and pacify it with cool thoughts. Keep the juices flowing by jangling around gently as you move. Go very light on the vices, such as carrying on in society. The social ramble ain't restful. Avoid running at all times. Don't look back. Something might be gaining on you.

"Don't look back." Mr. Paige saved the most important one for last. If we keep looking back at the past, we may become depressed about our failures or arrogant about our successes. We must look forward to new adventures and new successes.

CHAPTER 5

What About the Future?

EARLIER CHAPTERS have been directed to an analysis of your job, or any job, from the standpoint of the satisfaction it may give you and its suitability for you.

But what about the future? Is it time to rethink your career? You need only to study newspapers, magazine articles, and books to know that major forces are affecting the United States and the world's economies, and changes in the job picture are certain. Each year, thousands of jobs disappear and are never seen again, and thousands of new ones appear.

The economic boom of the late 1990s led to such high employment that the wages of even the lowest-paid workers topped the inflation level, according to an analysis of the Bureau of Labor Statistics data by the Economic Policy Institute. Most economic analysts feel that such good times will not return anytime soon.

Not only is change certain, it is taking place at a faster pace than in the past. Corporations are gobbling up other corporations through acquisition, often resulting in downsizing. Some of these acquisitions involve globalization. Another major factor is advancing technology.

New government regulations result in changes. Demographic shifts occur. Continued immigration from Mexico, for example, where many workers who travel north are low-skilled, results in changes in the makeup of the U.S. workforce.

Companies exist to meet their own and their customers' needs, and they change accordingly. These changes can include downsizing. It is important to confront the fact that today there is little predictability and not much job security. If you do not face these issues, you run the risk that in your work career you will be taken by surprise and blindsided.

Before you undertake the steps involved in searching for a job and getting hired, it is time for a cautionary note. Predicting the future is not easy. Football coach Lou Holtz recognized this when he said, "I'm dead certain my team is going to move the ball. I pray to God it's forward."

Here are some notable forecasts that foundered on the shoals of time:

Woodrow Wilson, 1906: "Nothing has spread socialistic feeling more than the use of the automobile . . . a picture of the arrogance of wealth."

Tom Watson, 1943: "I think there's a world market for about five computers."

Business Week, 1958: "With over fifty foreign cars already on sale here, the Japanese auto industry isn't likely to carve out a big slice of the U.S. market for itself."

Daryl F. Zanuck, 1946: "TV won't be able to hold on to any market it captures after the first six months. People will soon get tired of staring at a plywood box every night."

Henry Luce, 1956: "By 1980 all power (electric, atomic, solar) is likely to be virtually costless."

Analyze Industry Trends

If you are alert to changes in the marketplace and study their nature, you may exploit them and use them to your advantage. To analyze changing trends, first establish a benchmark against which to compare your company by studying the industry and the major changes that are taking place in it.

Which companies are becoming dominant? What are they doing that is enabling them to become leaders? How are they handling new developments? Are they causing them? Review their publications, annual reports, newsletters, advertising, and on-line information. Network with others in the industry.

Against this benchmark, evaluate your own company. Is it adjusting to new developments? Review its publications without naïveté, reading carefully between the lines.

A detailed method of sizing up your company and your future in it was given in Chapter 2, Evaluating Job Satisfaction. Direct this analysis to yourself by asking:

- What is happening to my profession (my specialty)?

- Do I run the risk of becoming obsolete?

- Is it better for me to remain in my career and master it, or should I be ready to switch careers if trends indicate I should?

Additional information is available from the Bureau of Labor Statistics at the address given in Chapter 1.

The Fastest-Growing Occupations

The Department of Labor report for the year 2000 on work in the twenty-first century lists the following as the fastest-growing occupations:

Computer engineers

Personal care and health

Computer support specialists

Health care aides

Database administrators

Physicians' assistants

Data-processing equipment repairs

Residential counselors

Dental hygienists

Securities and financial advisers

Desktop publishing specialists

Sales workers

Medical assistants

System analysts

Paralegals

Changes in population and demographics, diversity, and technology are among the major forces making for these changes in employment in the United States, says this report.

The Best-Paid Occupations

The ten occupations with the highest earnings are listed as:

Physicians

Dentists

Podiatrists

Aircraft pilots and flight engineers

Lawyers

Petroleum engineers

Physicists and astronomers

Engineering, natural science, and computer and
information systems managers

Optometrists

Aerospace engineers

Sources of Information

These data are from the U.S. Department of Labor publication
"Future Work: Trends and Challenges for Work in the Twenty-First
Century." The report is fascinating and authoritative but far too
long even to be excerpted here.

You can read this report online at www.dol.gov (type in "future
work report"), or phone for a copy of the report at: (202) 219-6001,
extension 123. You can also read a summary of the report, called
"Executive Summary," online at: www.dol.gov/asp/futurework/exec-
sum.htm.

Data on earnings by specific occupations from the Occupational
Employment Statistics (OES) survey can be obtained from:

Bureau of Labor Statistics
Office of Employment and Unemployment Statistics
Occupational Employment Statistics
2 Massachusetts Avenue NE, Room 4840
Washington, DC 21212-0001
(202) 691-6569
Internet: http://stats.bls.gov/oes and type in "Executive
Summary"

Researching a Job and an Industry

Your examination of trends and changes may have led you to identify a job that seems promising and about which you want to know

more. Or it may be that you are about to be interviewed for a job and you want to be fully informed about it so you can do well in the interview. In either case, here are the principal questions you ought to ask yourself and be able to answer:

- What are the available openings for this position?

- What are they likely to be in the future?

- What is the compensation level for entry positions and higher positions?

- What are the opportunities for promotion to higher positions?

- What background is required: education, training, experience?

- What personal qualities, characteristics, and skills do I need?

- What are the most satisfying aspects of the job? What is the downside?

- What is a typical day like?

- What is the future for the industry?

- How can I learn more about the industry and the job?

To secure answers, you should start by reading the appropriate business papers and by using the sources listed earlier in this chapter.

Online Educational Resources

This may be a good time to resume an incomplete or interrupted education or to go for a Master's degree. You may find it comforting, rewarding, supporting, and stabilizing once again to write papers, study for tests, and earn a degree.

If you choose this avenue, here is a list of Web sites that can make the transition back to college easier.

- **Student Loan Funding:** www.studentloanfunding.com

  This site, a subsidiary of Sallie Mae, guides you through the process of applying for PLUS, STAFFORD, and other loans. It also provides loan calculators to help you figure out how much you will need.

- **Internship Programs:** www.internshipprograms.com

  Here you can find internships in a variety of fields, including major corporations, nonprofit organizations, government, and others. You can also post your résumé, so that prospective employers can contact you.

- **AOL College Finder:** AOL Keyword: College Finder

  All you need to do is type the name of the college in which you are interested to get a description of everything from tuition to almost anything else you want to know about it. In addition, there is a decision guide to help you find the college most suitable for you.

- **U.S. News.com Education:** www.usnews.com/usnews/edu

  This is the well-known *U.S. News* ranking of colleges, containing also a great deal of descriptive information about the schools.

- **College Club:** www.collegeclub.com

  This is a particularly useful site even if you do not choose to continue your education. It includes information about how to conduct yourself during an interview, how to write good cover letters to accompany your résumé, and other tips for conducting job searches. It also contains an "Academics" channel link with information on a wide variety of college majors.

How to Pursue a Scholarship

Each year more than 25,000 companies, foundations, and institutions provide over 700,000 scholarships, yet you have to work pretty hard to get one.

One company, Coca-Cola, gives away 250 each year. What's so hard? There are approximately 117,000 applicants.

Get Information from the Web

- www.scholarships.com

  Here you fill out a questionnaire and are provided with a list of appropriate grants. The site searches over 600,000 scholarships. There is no fee, but they do turn over personal information to their marketing partners.

- www.scholarship-page.com

  This site lists dozens of scholarships around the country, with brief descriptions and information about how to contact them. They will also provide updates if you sign up for them.

- www.collegeboard.com

  These listings are based on the College Board's annual survey of financial aid programs.

- www.fastweb.com

  This is one of the earliest scholarship databases. The administrators of foundations continually update information at this site.

- www.fastaid.com

  After you complete a questionnaire, a search of their database comes up with appropriate scholarships.

- www.wiredscholar.com

  This is Sallie Mae's scholarship database and financial aid site.

The Application Procedure

Most scholarships are based on merit or on a mix of merit and financial need. Their eligibility requirements are severe, such as a requirement of specific grade-point averages. Search for which awards to pursue based on their requirements and your own academic track record. Be realistic. Application forms can be long and complicated. They may take fifteen to twenty hours to complete.

Many grants and scholarship foundations have missions. Make sure your approach and orientation are consistent and in harmony with the organization's mission by including one or two personal stories with relevant themes if you can do so appropriately.

Most awards are small, from $500 to $3,000. Therefore, you need to accumulate several awards to win significant money. There are usually fewer applicants for regional and local awards, so your chances of securing such scholarships may be better.

Dollars for Scholars is a national organization with about a thousand chapters. They are the control coordinators for community groups that provide scholarships. See if you can locate a chapter in or near your area and investigate what is available.

Tests

Will you need to take Scholastic Aptitude Test (SAT), Graduate Record Examination (GRE), or American College Test (ACT)? If so, there are a number of helpful resources.

- Number2.com: www.number2.com

  This free site is excellent for preparing for all three of the tests listed. You are given questions based on your skill level, a personalized home page for tracking progress, and reminder e-mails.

- *The Princeton Review*: www.review.com

  This site, also free, provides sample SAT tests and other assessment tests. They also offer online courses, including coaches, workshops, and multimedia lessons, at $399 to start and, for an additional $400, a live coach for your problem subjects.

* Kaplan Test Prep and Admissions: www.kaptest.com

  Free sample tests are provided, ranging from the SAT to the U.S. Medical Licensing Exam. You need to sign up for membership, but it is free, as are tips on strategies for taking the tests.

* Exam Web: www.examweb.com

  This site charges $225 for SAT preparation, for which you get hundreds of tutorials, exams, personalized feedback, and a tracking system. There are also fee programs for the LSAT (Law School Admission Test) and the GRE.

* Distance Learning Resource Network: www.dlrn.org

  This is the U.S. Department of Education's Web site. If offers a directory of online courses for children and adults.

* The International Distance Learning Course Finder: www.dlcoursefinder.com

  Thousands of distance learning courses are listed here. A directory is provided by country, subject, method of delivery, and other categories.

An MBA can cost up to $100,000 and two years of your life. Such questions arise as: Should I choose a cheaper public university or a more expensive prestigious private school? Can the cost of tuition and the lost income while at school be recouped, and how long will that take?

You can obtain answers to these and other questions by accessing a Web site provided by *Business Week* magazine (www.businessweek.com). Click on B.SCHOOLS. Click the header GETTING IN. Under that, click ROI CALCULATOR. Then choose the business schools you are considering. You will be asked to put in your salary, gender, home state, years of work experience, current employer's size by number of employees, undergraduate major, and career plan. When you have entered this information, click CALCULATE at the bottom of the screen. You will be able to download personalized statistics on:

- The amount of money you will have to invest (including lost income)

- Your estimated salary increases

- The years it will take to recoup the investment through salary increases

- Ten years' worth of estimated salary increases

- The annualized rate of return on the money you spent

For Older Workers

The growth projections for thousands of jobs are listed in the Bureau of Labor Statistics' *Occupational Outlook Handbook* (www.bls.gov/oco, and click on Occupational Handbook in left margin). For older workers, six fields seem especially promising:

Teaching

Nursing

Policing

Psychology

Financial planning

Information technology

CHAPTER **6**

Realizing Your Potential

Be nice to nerds. Chances are you'll end up working for one.

—*Bill Gates*

How do I get where I want to be? One approach is to go with the flow, to let events determine your future, to be passive and reactive, rather than proactive, and hope everything works out for you.

A different approach is to get a realistic picture of what you want in life and to establish goals and plans to get there. Of course, if good luck intervenes and accelerates the movement toward your goals, or even causes you to change them in the right direction, so much the better.

In talks to high school and college graduates, Bill Gates lists eleven things they did not learn in school. He talks about how politically correct feel-good teachings created a full generation of kids with no concept of reality and how this concept set them up for failure in the real world.

What Bill Gates tells college kids is this:

1. Life is not fair; get used to it.
2. The world won't care about your self-esteem. The world will expect you to accomplish something *before* you feel good about yourself.
3. You will *not* make $40,000 a year right out of high school. You won't be a vice president with a car phone until you earn both.
4. If you think your teacher is tough, wait until you get a boss. He doesn't have tenure.
5. Flipping burgers is not beneath your dignity. Your grandparents had a different word for burger flipping. They called it *opportunity*.
6. If you mess up, it's not your parents' fault, so don't whine about your mistakes, learn from them.
7. Before you were born, your parents weren't as boring as they are now. They got that way from paying your bills, cleaning your clothes, and listening to you talk about how cool you are. So before you save the rain forest from the parasites of your parents' generation, try delousing the closet in your own room.
8. Your school may have done away with winners and losers, but life has not. In some schools, they have abolished failing grades; they'll give you as many times as you want to get the right answer. This doesn't bear the slightest resemblance to *anything* in real life.
9. Life is not divided into semesters. You don't get summers off, and very few employers are interested in helping you find yourself. Do that on your own time.
10. Television is *not* real life. In real life, people actually have to leave the coffee shop and go to jobs.
11. Be nice to nerds. Chances are you'll end up working for one.

Influences on Goals

The Seasons of Life

Good luck cannot be counted on, change can. Twenty-year-olds, on their first job, are willing to be gofers and take direction from others, expecting it to be part of the training and developmental process. To many forty-year-olds, this is unacceptable. So in any consideration of the process of setting goals, what has been referred to as the seasons of a person's life must be taken into account.

The Interdependence of Vocational and Personal Needs

Adding to the fact that goal planning and goal setting are not simple is the fact that your vocational world and your personal world are interdependent and not capable of being separated. For example, if there are children and both parents have careers, whose career growth should dominate and which spouse should take over parental responsibilities and at what time? Or should day-care centers or children's caregivers be considered? Is such a decision acceptable to the parents from the standpoint of the children's development?

These and many other questions suggest the need for considerable thinking about career plans, family plans, and lifestyle plans.

Your Priorities

A good place to start is to evaluate the dominant forces in your life and the priority to give to each.

For example, to one person, the definition of success is based on such factors as job title, compensation, status, and the potential for continued upward movement in the company. But another person says, "I'm happy with my job and its location, and I don't want to be promoted or to move." Such a person is saying, For me, factors other than job success are more important to my happiness.

Sometimes the fact that we constantly think and talk about our jobs obscures other more personal factors, especially because they may not be so easy to define and identify.

The following exercise may help you to clarify and evaluate the relationships, institutions, and concepts that are important in your life. Once you have done that, you are likely to be better able to set your lifetime goals on the basis of the importance you want these factors to hold in the future.

Setting Priorities

Step One

Here are eight priorities that are important, in different degrees, to most people: Family, Health, Religion, Job, Friends, Recognition, Money, Home.

Add others you feel should be included. The purpose of this exercise is to establish the degree of importance, to you, of these priorities.

Step Two

On page 68 is a map of the United States and on page 69 is a key to the cities on the map. Pretend you live in Kansas City, roughly the center of the country. Using a black felt-tipped pen, place a dot at Kansas City.

Now indicate those priorities that are most important to you by assigning them to cities close to Kansas City. Place a dot to indicate those nearby cities. Label the priorities they represent.

Less important priorities should be located farther away. The less important you consider a priority to be, the farther the city to which you assign that priority should be from the home city, Kansas City.

Thus priorities that are most important will be clustered in cities near Kansas City. This can be considered your present situation, where you are right now.

Step Three

Go back to the list of your priorities and consider their probable importance to you in five years, if things work out as you would like in your career program.

Using a different color felt-tip pen, relocate these probably revised priorities on the same map in relationship to Kansas City, putting those with highest priority closest to Kansas City and using greater distance from Kansas City to indicate decreased importance of the priority.

Step Four

Using yet another color felt-tip pen, relocate the priorities as you think they would be if you just let things alone without any planning or effort on your part.

Now look at the map.

- Which factors changed location (1) after five years under ideal circumstances, and (2) after five years if you let things alone?

- What new understanding did you gain from this exercise?

- What do you need to do to bring about the ideal situation you marked on the map?

Based on the insights derived from the map, enlarge your thinking by listing the specific career goals you would like to attain in five years. Be as concrete as possible. For example: "I would like to be a district manager in my present company"; "I would like to be earning $_____"; and so on.

_____

_____

_____

_____

_____

_____

Map of the United States with Cities

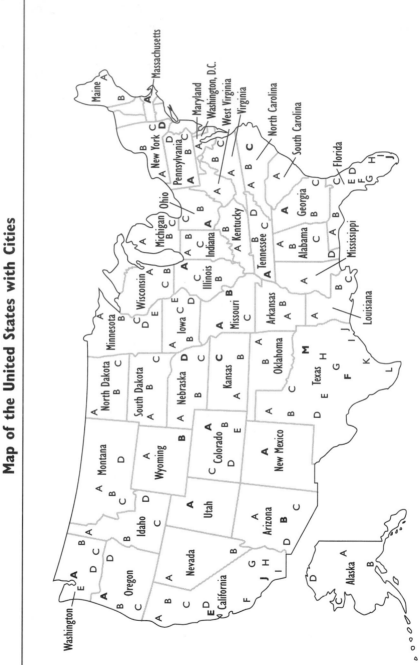

Alabama
A—Huntsville, B—Birmingham, C—Montgomery, **D—Mobile**

Alaska
A—Fairbanks, **B—Anchorage,** C—Nome, D—Barrow

Arizona
A—Flagstaff, **B—Phoenix,** C—Tucson, D—Yuma

Arkansas
A—Hot Springs, B—Little Rock

California
A—Eureka, B—Redding, C—Sacramento, D—Stockton, **E—San Francisco,** F—San Luis Obisbo, G—Barstow, H—San Bernardino, I—San Diego, **J—Los Angeles**

Colorado
A—Denver, B—Colorado Springs, C—Grand Junction, D—Durango, E—Pueblo

Florida
A—Panama City, B—Tallahassee, C—Jacksonville, D—Daytona Beach, E—Orlando, F—Tampa, G—St. Petersburg, H—West Palm Beach, I—Ft. Lauderdale, J—Miami

Georgia
A—Atlanta, B—Columbus, C—Augusta

Idaho
A—Coeur d'Alene, B—Boise, C—Twin Falls, D—Pocatello

Illinois
A—Chicago, B—Springfield, C—Peoria

Indiana
A—Gary, B—Wayne, **C—Indianapolis**

Iowa
A—Sioux City, B—Council Bluffs, C—Cedar Rapids, D—Davenport, **E—Des Moines**

Kansas
A—Dodge City, B—Wichita, **C—Topeka**

Kentucky
A—Louisville, B—Lexington

Louisiana
A—Shreveport, B—Baton Rouge, **C—New Orleans**

Maine
A—Bangor, B—Portland

Maryland
A—Baltimore

Massachusetts
A—Boston

Michigan
A—Grand Rapids, B—Lansing, C—Detroit

Minnesota
A—Ely, B—Duluth, C—St. Paul, D—Minneapolis, E—Rochester

Mississippi
A—Jackson

Missouri
A—Kansas City, B—St. Louis, C—Springfield

Montana
A—Great Falls, B—Helena, D—Butte, E—Billings

Nebraska
A—Scottsbluff, B—North Platte, **C—Omaha,** D—Lincoln

Nevada
A—Reno, B—Las Vegas

New Mexico
A—Albuquerque

New York
A—Buffalo, B—Syracuse, C—Albany, **D—New York**

North Dakota
A—Williston, B—Bismark, C—Fargo

North Carolina
A—Winston-Salem, B—Greensboro, **C—Raleigh**

Ohio
A—Cincinnati, B—Columbus, C—Toledo

Oklahoma
A—Tulsa, B—Oklahoma City

Oregon
A—Portland, B—Eugene, D—Pendleton, E—Grand Pass

Pennsylvania
A—Pittsburgh, B—Harrisburg, C—Philadelphia, D—Scranton

Puerto Rico
A—San Juan

South Carolina
A—Columbus

South Dakota
A—Rapid City, B—Pierre, C—Sioux Falls

Tennessee
A—Memphis, B—Nashville, C—Chattanooga, D—Knoxville

Texas
A—Amarillo, B—Lubbock, C—Wichita Falls, D—Odessa, E—San Angelo, **F—San Antonio,** G—Austin, H—Waco, I—Houston, J—Galveston, K—Corpus Christi, L—Brownsville, **M—Dallas**

Utah
A—Salt Lake City

Virginia
A—Roanoke, B—Richmond, C—Norfolk

Washington, D.C.

Washington
A—Seattle, B—Spokane, C—Walla Walla, D—Yakima, E—Olympia

West Virginia
A—Charleston

Wisconsin
A—Green Bay, B—Milwaukee, C—Madison

Wyoming
A—Casper, **B—Cheyenne**

List your goals for family and social relationships, again being as specific as possible.

_____

_____

_____

_____

Now list the skills, abilities, and other personal attributes you would like to achieve through personal development in the next five years.

_____

_____

_____

_____

CHAPTER 7

The Stages in a Person's Life

If the son does not turn out to be a better man than the father, probably both have failed.

—*Old Chinese adage*

CONSIDER A YOUNG man in his early twenties. He has a great taste for adventure and loves to travel. He does not hold on to a job very long. He is not anxious to undertake responsibilities. On those jobs he has so far held, he is not sure he enjoys daily work routines or having a boss. He may not think he has so far encountered the right job for him.

Picture that same young man at thirty-five. He is married and has a child. He is sober, serious, and anxious to succeed at his job and make a good impression on his bosses. He is pretty sure he wants to stay in his present field of work and keeps alert to advancement opportunities, either in his company or in others.

This is not an unusual scenario and suggests (1) that there is a close relationship between the stages in one's career and the stages in one's life, and (2) that with advancing years there are psychological changes as well as physical ones. If one becomes more mature emotionally, greater stability, self-confidence, and self-reliance will also emerge.

Many studies have been conducted to understand the stages in a person's career and the stages in a person's life. In career planning and goal setting, and in determining the soundness of a person's satisfaction or dissatisfaction with his or her job, sufficient and proper consideration must be given to the changes that occur with growing older. You are not the same person at forty that you were at twenty, not psychologically, emotionally, physically, or in your possession of job-related skills and abilities.

Career Stages

One important study indicates that organizations expect employees to progress through four career stages.

Stage 1: Employees are involved in being trained, usually by their supervisors, on whom they are dependent. They are expected to follow directions and to develop the necessary skills for their jobs.

Stage 2: There should be growth in employee self-reliance and a growth in their ability to work with others in the organization. Employees should be less dependent on the boss.

Stage 3: Not only should employees in this stage of development be relatively self-sufficient, they should also begin to provide training and support for others.

Stage 4: Now they should be involved in the organization's growth and providing leadership.

Again, certain conclusions emerge. Apparently, continued growth in the job requires more than growth in the abilities and skills needed in the job. Successful people need to show the kind of psychological growth that moves them from being dependent on others to self-reliance and independence. This, in turn, leads to job growth.

Older people who are still in junior positions in many cases are believed by their companies to have failed to grow in psychological maturity. They may have acquired the necessary skills but not the necessary independence and willingness to take responsibility for the work of others. Not only do they fail to advance, they may, under some circumstances, risk being encouraged to leave, or even fired, to make room for younger people with more promising potential.

Life Stages

Since we have seen that career stages and life stages are linked, it is worthwhile to examine what research suggests are the stages in people's lives. This is especially important to understand because, as we have seen, career progress depends not only on growth in job skills and abilities but also on growth in maturity and psychological development.

Here are the life stages, according to extensive research:

Adolescence: This period, ages fifteen to twenty-two, is characterized by the fact that the individual is usually unmarried and is busy establishing his or her individuality, distinct from parents. The beginnings of independence take place here, but there is still a serious need for support from adults, usually parents. As it is written in the Torah, "Train not thy children in thine own way, for they are born for a different time."

Transition to Adulthood: During this period, ages twenty-two to thirty, the individual enters marriage, learning to consider the spouse's needs, and make decisions about family, children, and lifestyle.

Adulthood: In this period, ages thirty to thirty-eight, the demands of parenthood, in addition to adjusting to the spouse's needs, dominate the psychological concerns.

Transition to Midlife: By ages thirty-eight to forty-five, there is a need for coping with the considerable challenges of dealing with adolescent children. Also, at this stage, time is beginning to run out for making major changes in one's life.

Middle Adulthood: Ages forty-five to fifty-five bring substantial change. Children have grown up and left home for college and marriage. Parents age or die, and there is less focus on children and more need for establishing a closer spousal relationship.

Transition into Late Life: At ages fifty-five to sixty-two, there is less focus on work and more focus on anticipated retirement. Toward that end, consideration is given to activities, hobbies, and relationships with others. As grandparents, some attention shifts toward helping children, financially and otherwise, to cope with *their* children.

Late Life: By age sixty-two and over, grandchildren have become adolescents or adults. Increased illnesses create financial and emotional demands, and the need for a realistic but healthy adjustment to the increased awareness of death is needed.

One warning: The greatest emphasis in this research has been on the stages in a middle-class white man's life. There has been some research on the development of African American men and on women but not nearly as much as on white men. Also, the "typical" families studied were stable ones, with children, and with one spouse, usually the wife, not working full time. With the increased frequency of divorces, single parents, remarriages, stepparents, and both parents working fulltime, these models of life stages may be less typical than was originally believed.

Summary

In considering your own career and goal planning, and taking into account these career and life stages, it is important to note that there is considerable evidence that employees in their twenties are often dissatisfied with their jobs, compensation, and bosses, though pleased with their relationships with coworkers and the opportunities their jobs give them to develop their skills and abilities and gain experience.

There is a greater level of satisfaction with people in their thirties, a decrease in the thirty-eight- to forty-five-year-old stage, and, at age forty-five, an upturn again in job satisfaction. Some older workers seem to show less job commitment and involvement.

With this in mind, part of your analysis of your own job happiness and satisfaction should include consideration of whether dissatisfaction, if any, is caused by the job itself, the work, the surroundings, or simply by those feelings that are typical of a career stage.

For younger readers, the period up to about age thirty is critical in career and goal planning. It is at that time that important decisions are made, whether to marry and whom to marry, whether to have children, whether to change careers, go back to school, and so on. Some of these decisions may be hard to reverse, others irreversible.

CHAPTER 8

The Causes of Job Success and Failure

Oh wad some power the giftie gie us
To see oursels as ithers see us.

—*Robert Burns*

SOMETIMES IT IS valuable to step back and consider how informed and knowledgeable people—human resource specialists, employers, job counselors, employment agents, search firm executives—look at the qualities that make for job success or failure.

What, then, most frequently leads to failure or dissatisfactions on or with the job? Which abilities or deficiencies have the most impact on job success?

A word in extensive current use that encompasses a variety of abilities and qualities is *competencies*. This chapter discusses three kinds of competencies: specific job competencies, transferable competencies, and personal competencies.

Specific Job Competencies

By definition, these competencies have to do with a specific job. A simple example in an office setting might involve the ability to use software programs on a computer, word processing, working on spreadsheets, and handling invoicing. For a specialized automobile mechanic, it would be the ability to repair transmission systems.

In more complex jobs, district sales management, for example, it would have to do with the ability to recruit and screen sales candidates, execute performance appraisals, and solve local sales problems.

Because specific job competencies are by definition specific to a particular job, they cannot be transferred to a different kind of work. Only rarely are they a cause of failure on the job. The selection policies in most companies tend to screen out people who cannot successfully master the specific job competencies they need.

Transferable Competencies

This name is also descriptive. Though acquired in order to do one job, transferable competencies are applicable to other jobs and situations. Examples of transferable competencies in such jobs as district sales management and product and brand management include the abilities to conduct a meeting, persuade others, listen to a subordinate, and conduct a counseling interview.

In another example, a computer mechanic or technician would be expected to use certain tools or understand the principles of telecommunications.

While transferable competencies are more complex and perhaps more difficult to acquire than specific job competencies, they are also not a major cause of job failure.

Personal Competencies

Personal competencies are the ones that frequently cause trouble, particularly for those in people-oriented positions, including high-level executive positions.

Often, employees with good ideas, whose decisions and concepts are sound from the standpoint of specific and transferable job competencies, find themselves in trouble and conflict with their peers and superiors because of personal competencies. In fact, failures in the way people function at the level of personal competencies often adversely affect their job performance, even though they may be entirely competent at the specific and transferable competency levels.

It is generally believed that personal competencies are acquired by an individual at a very early age. How a child deals with other people, both with peers and with authority figures, determines how he or she, as an adult, will deal with colleagues and bosses. How the child develops the ability to deal with the environment, learns to regard himself or herself as OK or not OK, and learns how to take criticism has an obvious connection to what kind of adult he or she will become and, therefore, what kind of an employee. In short, personal competencies have to do with how an individual has learned, since childhood, to deal with people, with the world, with life.

Openness, Spontaneity, and Naturalness

Openness, spontaneity, and naturalness are all words used to express the competency to deal with others and with the world in an open and natural way. This is the equivalent of an "I'm OK" life script. In everyday conversation, this would be described as "What you see is who he (or she) is."

The opposite of this competency is role-playing, pretending to be what you are not. Usually, others see through this, and as a result your credibility is undermined.

> The company president was talking to his managers. "What we need around here is someone with some guts, who'll speak his honest convictions without fear of retaliation. Like that young kid who used to be here—what was his name again?"

The personal competency involved here is the ability to know when we are role-playing and what there is in the situation or our perception of the situation that causes us to do so. This ability enables us to quit role-playing and to be open once again.

Ability to Know How We Affect Others

One of the most interesting phenomena in interpersonal relations is the inability of some individuals to achieve realistic insights into their effect on others. Thus, for example, most of us have witnessed the abrasive person who has no idea at all that he or she consistently antagonizes the group with whom he or she must work.

To lack this insight, this ability, is to encounter difficulty in changing one's behavior for the better.

Ability to Improve Behavior

This competency is related to the foregoing one. Some people receive and even solicit feedback from others on their shortcomings and are able to overcome them. Other people close their eyes to such information, deny they have a problem, or act in other defensive ways.

Relationship with the Boss

Early in our lives, we develop characteristic ways of dealing with authority figures (first our parents, later our teachers, then our bosses). Some people learn to be dependent, even subservient; others become rebellious; and still others manage to have healthy, interdependent relationships.

Successful employees have the competency to evaluate, realistically, their relationships with their bosses, so that they can modify their own behaviors and understand their bosses' behavior toward themselves.

Relationships with Others

The ability willingly to expose oneself to contact with others is, of course, especially important in essentially people-oriented jobs. To be cold, austere, remote, and reserved is to remove oneself from an essential part of the work.

Some students of human behavior believe that people who assume a remote position from others may sometimes do so for fear that if others got to know them really well they would be seen to be unworthy or unlikable.

Ability to Deal with Conflict

Conflict is part of life—inevitable, normal, and to be encountered in almost all settings. Some people deny this and flee from conflict. Other people fight and try to give better than they get. Still others look for someone—an ally—to help them. These are all patterns learned in childhood.

Employees are not insulated from conflict. The needed competency is to recognize the proper way to respond to a particular conflict situation and have the repertoire to employ that way of responding.

Ability to Give Feedback to Others

One way of expressing caring and feeling for other people is to give them feedback on how their behaviors are seen by others. In some positions, especially in supervisory and managerial positions, this is frequently a duty and a responsibility of the job.

Some people who lack this ability simply run away from situations they could deal with or handle in more healthy ways. They refrain from giving feedback at all. With others, the feedback they give is full of moralistic judgments and unsought advice, advice the person gives to meet his or her own needs, not the other person's.

The ability to give feedback clearly and with skill is one of the most important personal competencies.

Ability to Judge Self-Worth

One of the abilities apparently learned early in childhood is to judge accurately where we are strong and where we are weak. Related to this ability is the ability to place in proper perspective the ups and downs we all experience in self-esteem.

People who have developed this ability can see themselves accurately, know what they are good at and weak at, and accept that status. They can also step back from the highs and lows of feelings of self-worth, recognize that actual worth differs from these fluctuations of feelings, and even evaluate the factors that led to the fluctuations.

Can Personal Competencies Be Developed on the Job?

A large body of behavioral scientists maintains that these personal competencies begin to be developed, or fail to develop, early in life. And they believe, also, that as people grow older, it usually becomes more difficult to wean people from these established behaviors and in favor of new ones. This is because every time a person behaves in a certain way and perceives the results of that behavior as leading to success, he or she receives positive reinforcement that this is the right way to behave.

The more times the individual receives positive reinforcement for actions taken, the more such actions become a behavioral pattern and the more difficult it is to change to a new behavior. Thus it is probably a valid generalization to say that the younger you are, the easier it is to modify and develop your own personal competencies.

Finally, from the standpoint of the reader, it is important to realize that no person has fully developed and mastered all these competencies.

The important and realistic viewpoint for any individual is to investigate and assess the extent to which he or she owns these competencies, to learn more about himself or herself with respect to them, and to move toward slow and steady growth in these competencies, and thus toward becoming a more fulfilled person.

PART III

The Importance of Self-Assessment

When you get what you want in both power and pelf,
When you're queen or king for a day,
Then go to the mirror and look at yourself,
To see what that one would say.

For it isn't your parent or husband or wife
Whose judgment upon you must pass.
The person whose verdict counts most in your life
Is the one staring back from the glass.

That's the one you must please; never mind all the rest,
This one's with you clear to the end,

And you've passed your most difficult, dangerous test
If the one in the glass is your friend.

Play the role of the big shot and earn quite a sum
And get more than your share of the pie.
But the one in the glass will say you're a bum
If your look is not straight in the eye.

You can fool the whole world down the pathway of years
And get pats on the back as you pass,
But your final reward will be heartaches and tears,
If you've cheated the one in the glass.

—*"The Person in the Mirror"*

CHAPTER **9**

Who Am I?

What lies behind us and what lies before us are tiny
matters compared to what lies within us.
—*Ralph Waldo Emerson*

IT TAKES NO great stretch to see that an understanding of "Who Am
I?" is essential in any consideration of your career and vocational
choices.

As far back as 1942, renowned psychiatrist Karen Horney
wrote, in her book *Self-Analysis*:

Attempts at self-analysis can be important, in the first place,
for the individual him or herself. Such an endeavor gives him
a chance for self-realization.

By this I mean not only the development of special gifts
that he or she may have been inhibited from utilizing, but

also, even more important, the development of potentialities as a strong and integrated human being.

Some of the advantages of self-analysis are these:

- It forces you to consider the positions you have had in the past, whether they were a good match for who you are, and therefore to decide whether you should continue in those directions or consider a change in career decisions in the future.

- This is, in turn, a catalyst for making that change, if that is your decision and other options are open to you.

- If a career change seems warranted, it encourages you to try to experiment and test new positions consistent with who you are and even to experiment and test your choices.

- Finally, it requires you, perhaps for the first time, to study what your long-term career outlook should be and reinforces the conclusion that you alone are responsible for managing your life.

It is comforting to think that in a world that is constantly changing, we remain basically the same, unchanged in any major degree. But it is just because we are so close to ourselves that we have trouble seeing ourselves objectively.

Nor can parents always be relied on to tell us, objectively, who we are. Studies have shown that parental attitudes toward themselves and toward others, including their children, tend to change. Parents tend to develop more rigid moral attitudes and behavior and more severe ethical thinking as they grow older. Not only may the treatment a person gets from parents change over the years, it is also true that children coming into the family at different times in the lives of parents get different treatment. In fact, birth order—the child's rank in the family as first-born, second-born, third-born, and so on—affects how he or she is treated and how the parents judge his or her behavior.

If we are to understand ourselves, we need to have some objectivity. Since we can't stand outside ourselves in the way we can stand and perceive others, we need to fall back, instead, on some kind of device or technique that will permit us to see ourselves, perhaps from a new point of view.

The devices described in the following four chapters will deal with these factors. They are presented in such a way as to help you measure and analyze these aspects of your makeup:

- Values

- Interests

- Personality

- Skills, abilities, and job preferences

But just because it is difficult to see ourselves as others see us, it is important to have some objective "others"—who know you well—to provide you with feedback regarding the accuracy of your perceptions of your values, interests, personality, skills, abilities, and job preferences.

CHAPTER **10**

Measure Your Values

"Who are *you?*" said the Caterpillar. . . . Alice replied, rather shyly, "I—I hardly know, Sir, just at present—at least I know who I *was* when I got up this morning, but I think I must have been changed several times since then."

—Lewis Carroll

GETTING TO KNOW yourself is the first phase of career planning, and getting to know your values is an important first step.

Values are important parts of our personality and thinking systems. They involve the way we look at life. Some students of values say they are life's driving forces.

All of us want to get as much out of life as we can. And all of us have, at one time or other, asked ourselves, "What do I want out of life?" "What is important to me?" "How do I define happiness?"

Once you have some answers, once you know something about your values, you're better able to set up job goals and better able to read your attitudes toward travel, relocation, and moving the family. Consider these groups of very rich people.

- Some regard their careers as a great success, an accomplishment that other people ought to recognize. They have a persistent urge for recognition.

- Others never stop achieving. Having expressed great satisfaction with their past achievements, they expect equal satisfaction from future ones. With more money than they will ever need, they are no longer primarily motivated by money, except as a symbol of achievement.

- Still others, with a large bump of altruism in their makeup, enjoy helping others with their advice and sometimes their philanthropies.

- Finally, a fourth group is frankly materialistic. These people build museums, travel, and buy expensive sport and entertainment apparatus. What they want out of life is the continued satisfaction of their material desires.

Research indicates that values are learned beliefs. Individuals learn them from family, religion, peers, educators, experiences, and the culture in general. Values are part of our personality and our cognitive systems: they direct how we act and how we think and seem to be stable over a considerable period of time. It therefore becomes clear that people should not favorably consider positions that require them to act or think in ways that conflict with their values.

This chapter provides a two-part approach to measuring your values. First is identifying your personal wants and values, and second is an inventory that will help you to understand five important value categories: theoretical, economic, aesthetic, social, and political. Clearly these aren't the only values we hold, but they are especially relevant to occupational choices. After you've completed and scored the values inventory, we'll explain what your scores represent.

Identifying Your Personal Wants and Values

Work satisfies many of your personal wants and values, but they are not all equally important.

Here is a list of twenty values. Select the five that are most important to you in your career and put a plus (+) on the line to the left. Then select the five that are the least important and put a minus ( ) on the line to the left.

___ Independence, autonomy, freedom

___ Time with the family, family happiness

___ Power, influence, and control over others

___ Fun work, pleasure, free time

___ Self-fulfillment, full use of potential

___ Freedom from money worry, economic security

___ Altruism, assisting others/society, helpfulness

___ Friendship, affiliation, closeness to others

___ Status, prestige, respect, visibility, recognition

___ Structure, clear rules, freedom from chaos and instability

___ Integrity, acting in accordance with beliefs, honesty

___ Innovation, creativity, inventiveness

___ Teamwork, working with others, cooperation

___ Risk taking, competitive challenge, adventure

___ Leadership, directing others

___ Gaining knowledge, growing in education

___ Upward mobility, advancement, promotion

___ Responsibility, being accountable for results

___ Geographical location

___ Climate

Look over your results. Is there some consistency among those values that are important to you? Can you come to some conclusions regarding those that are least important?

Keep these insights in mind when you compare them with the results of the next exercise.

Are the results similar? If no, in what ways do they differ and can you account for their differences?

The Values Inventory

Each of the following twenty groups begins with a letter of the alphabet, from A through T. Each group contains three numbered statements. For each of the following statements in a group, place a 3 by the statement that is most important to you, a 2 by the statement that is less important to you, and a 1 by the remaining statement. Thus each group of three statements will have only one rated 3, one rated 2, and one rated 1.

A: ___ 1. I would vote for legislators who support efforts to encourage people to pay more attention to human rights.

___ 2. If I were a professor, the subject I would most like to teach would be science.

___ 3. The trade shows and expositions I most like to attend are those that deal with marketable products.

B: ___ 1. I favor most the kind of education that teaches students to be successful and prosperous.

___ 2. The best kind of hobby for me is to develop expertise in some type of skill.

___ 3. I enjoy reading and learning about famous painters and musicians.

C: ___ 1. If I had the ability, I would like to perform in a symphony orchestra as a member or soloist.

___ 2. I believe that compassion and sympathy are among the finest qualities of character.

___ 3. Basic pure science will, in the long run, prove to be of the greatest benefit to society.

D: ___ 1. I would like to study the latest research in psychology.

___ 2. I enjoy reading about the stock market, advertising, and real estate.

___ 3. I would enjoy being in a position to lead or influence public opinion.

E: ___ 1. I prefer a job as a line manager with some authority rather than a job as staff manager.

___ 2. I tend to be interested in the architectural aspects and beautiful features of new buildings.

___ 3. I would enjoy volunteer work in an educational or social service agency.

F: ___ 1. The principal characteristic of people I admire is that they like to help others.

___ 2. Pure scientists like Albert Einstein and Marie Curie have contributed the most to society.

___ 3. The greatness of Van Gogh's paintings is evidenced in the large sums of money they command when sold.

G: ___ 1. The basic purpose of science should be to make discoveries that can be directly applied to practical uses.

___ 2. I would like to be a leader of people in some enterprise.

___ 3. In reading prose or poetry, I am more influenced by its literary style than by its message.

H: ___ 1. I am moved at occasions like graduations or inaugurations by the finery and splendor of the event.

___ 2. I consider humanitarians like Mother Teresa and Albert Schweitzer among the greatest contributors to mankind.

___ 3. I believe that certain mathematicians and scientists, though they may be unknown to the general public, will ultimately be shown to have done the most for society.

I: ___ 1. I enjoy reading the science section of a newspaper or magazine more than most other sections.

___ 2. I believe the financial and stock market sections of a newspaper or magazine are the most important and interesting.

___ 3. I would like my child to be good at competitive sports.

J: ___ 1. A nation's policy should be to do things to gain importance and high regard worldwide.

___ 2. A person who works all week would benefit from attending concerts on the weekend.

___ 3. A country should be judged favorably if it provides for its poor, sick, and elderly citizens.

K: ___ 1. Public schools should make a greater effort to teach students about social problems.

___ 2. If I could make a grant to a university, it would be for the development of their scientific research resources.

___ 3. If I had a summer-long vacation, I would like to spend it learning about some aspect of business.

L: ___ 1. It is important that appropriate government agencies be set up to stimulate the development of business.

___ 2. If circumstances and conditions were right, I would love to be a successful politician.

___ 3. If I had the opportunity, I would like to aid in the establishment of a classical orchestra or a museum.

M: ___ 1. I would like to be a writer of articles on the arts, interior decoration, gardens, and so on.

___ 2. I most admire churches that do good works and encourage charitable activities.

___ 3. I would like to participate in physics, biology, or chemistry research.

N: ___ 1. Given the opportunity, I tend to choose reading material about the great thinkers and philosophers.

___ 2. As I read the newspapers, I concentrate my attention on business and financial news.

___ 3. I enjoy lectures on the successes or failures of different forms of government.

O: ___ 1. The historical figures I most like to read about are military leaders like Napoleon.

___ 2. I would like to be the literary or art or entertainment critic for a newspaper.

___ 3. A job such as human resources director would greatly interest me.

P: ___ 1. If I had the time and money, I would open a hospice for the terminally ill.

___ 2. I enjoy conversations about the latest discoveries in genetics, antibiotics, or some other aspect of science.

___ 3. I most favor those political leaders who endorse and bring about practical results.

Q: ___ 1. Given the opportunity, I would like to be involved in banking or in a stock brokerage company.

___ 2. I would like to be a winner or leading figure in some athletic activity.

___ 3. I tend to choose places to visit where I can admire the beautiful scenery.

R: ___ 1. When I travel, I like to visit museums and art galleries.

___ 2. If I had the means, I would like to establish a good facility for Alzheimer patients.

___ 3. If I had training, I would like to participate in research to find a cure for cancer.

S: ___ 1. I enjoy a movie that tries to get at the truth behind some controversial event.

___ 2. If I could afford it, I would buy some of Monet's paintings because they are sure to appreciate in value.

___ 3. If circumstances permitted it, I would like to be a senator or a member of the president's cabinet.

T: ___ 1. I can empathize with a climber of Mount Everest because it means triumphing over very difficult conditions.

___ 2. The best kind of financial donation is toward the establishment, expansion, or maintenance of a museum or symphony orchestra.

___ 3. The best kind of financial donation is to a charity that directly helps the poor, sick, and elderly.

Scoring the Values Inventory

Transfer the ratings you gave each of the items on the values inventory to the appropriate items that follow. Total the scores in each column and enter them on the last line.

Theoretical Values	Economic Values	Aesthetic Values	Social Values	Political Values
S1 _____	S2 _____	T2 _____	T3 _____	T1 _____
N1 _____	N2 _____	O2 _____	O3 _____	O1 _____
I2 _____	I2 _____	J2 _____	J3 _____	J1 _____
D1 _____	D2 _____	E2 _____	E3 _____	E1 _____
R3 _____	Q1 _____	R1 _____	R2 _____	S3 _____
M3 _____	L1 _____	M1 _____	M2 _____	N3 _____
H3 _____	G1 _____	H1 _____	H2 _____	I3 _____
C3 _____	B1 _____	C1 _____	C2 _____	D3 _____
P2 _____	P3 _____	Q3 _____	P1 _____	Q2 _____
K2 _____	K3 _____	L3 _____	K1 _____	L2 _____
F2 _____	F3 _____	G3 _____	F1 _____	G2 _____
A2 _____	A3 _____	B3 _____	A1 _____	B2 _____
Totals _____	_____	_____	_____	_____

Theoretical Values

To people with theoretical values, truth is all-important. They enjoy chasing the truth; they possess a love of learning. To them, truth is much more important than what is practical or beautiful. They tend to value activities like research and the academic and like positions such as chemist, biologist, physicist, and mathematician.

In business, people who have strong theoretical values may choose to work in market research. But unless they also have other, more practical values, they may be inclined to work toward the discovery of truth but pay little attention to its practical application. They may also lack an interest in leadership occupations.

Economic Values

People with an economic orientation like financial and material rewards. They tend to be utilitarian, caring most about what works, what is practical. When presented with a new idea, their first question may be, "How do you use this?" hence they tend toward the business world, in occupations involving production, advertising, sales, marketing, credit, and the consumption of goods and services.

When combined with high theoretical values, strong economic values could lead one to find practical truths. In fact, when a person has both strong economic and theoretical values, sometimes great accomplishments result.

People with economic values often enjoy occupations involving leadership and speaking activities. In short, this person represents the typical American businessperson.

Aesthetic Values

Beauty and the arts are important to people who have strong aesthetic values. This does not mean they are necessarily themselves creative or artistically talented. Rather, they are chiefly interested in the artistic experiences in life.

In the business world, they enjoy activities such as, for example, interior design or perhaps the artistic side of advertising and packaging. Such a position would be especially suitable if they also have economic values.

Aesthetic values may also tend to drive one's avocation rather than one's career choices.

Social Values

People with strong social values are the altruists of society. They care about people and want to help them. Sometimes they are the do-gooders.

You can find people with these values in occupations like teaching, coaching, social work, and counseling. Generally, these people do not highly value the theoretical.

Political Values

Political-values people are not necessarily involved in the field of politics but are associated with a desire for power. They look for prestige, control, influence. They are strongly interested in advancement, and when they are members of clubs and organizations look ultimately for positions of leadership in them. It is therefore not surprising that leaders in a variety of fields have high political values.

Understanding Your Values

When you review your scores based on your responses to the values inventory, you may very well find that you score high in several values. Here are some examples:

Political and economic: Such a combination is generally seen as that of the typical American businessperson. Staff positions may not satisfy people with this combination of values. However, line positions appeal both to their economic drive and their political value.

Aesthetic and economic: These people are concerned with the beautiful and artistic, but also with the practical and useful.

Theoretical and social: Such an individual may, for example, use mathematics and statistics to evaluate those social programs that are most beneficial for people.

Theoretical and economic: These individuals may look for discoveries through science that have practical value and can be applied.

Social and economic: These individuals would, for example, tend to favor those economic programs that would benefit people.

Political and theoretical: These individuals may use their knowledge as a way to exert influence over people. In their leadership roles, they may be said to be "experts."

Political and social: People with this combination of values welcome having power and using it to benefit people.

How Values Influence Career Choices

Let's look at some of the ways values may influence your career and job choices. Keep in mind that people with different combinations of values are functioning successfully and happily in all kinds of jobs, so don't be overly concerned if your value profile doesn't exactly match the values of those who typically hold the job you want. Just use the information to add to your personal database for decision making.

We have seen that the typical values of the American businessperson are economic and political. Holding such values does not necessarily affect job success and achievement. Some people achieve job success in business with other values. Values are more likely to affect one's satisfaction with the job or feelings of self-fulfillment rather than one's success.

A person who holds high aesthetic and high economic values might be very happy in a position such as package design, where the combination of the ability to provide a package with an attractive appearance that invites the customer to buy is necessary.

If a person combines high theoretical and high economic values, a couple of possibilities would be product management and market research.

Generally speaking, a person with strong social values might find some of the responsibilities of management to be difficult.

For example, a person who wishes to help others may experience conflict or even psychological pain if he or she has to discipline, fire, or otherwise "hurt" a subordinate.

Summary

Knowing something about your values is important in connection with your choice of a career. People tend to search for an occupation that is favorable to their drives and values and will usually find there people who are similar to themselves.

In considering the positions you explore and toward which you are favorably oriented, investigate whether they are likely to provide you with the important values you defined in the study. And, of course, consider also whether they are relatively free of the values you discovered are least important to you.

After scoring the inventory, you may find that you have no high values—or no low ones. These results, scores that are either high or low in all or most areas (or even in the middle) suggest that your values have not yet crystallized and you may need more time to establish your values more definitely. This is especially true for younger people.

How your values affect your career choices is highly individual. It's important to know what your values are so that you can evaluate possible careers and jobs to see whether the activities required match your values or are in conflict with them. If the job duties seem to be in conflict with your values, you might want to explore those responsibilities carefully and examine whether you would be happy in such a job.

CHAPTER **11**

Measure Your Interests

IF ONLY WE could try out different jobs for a number of years to see if we enjoy them and are good at them, and then have those years erased from our lives and our records, this chapter would be unnecessary. Since that is not the case, we need to try other approaches to help us make career and vocational decisions.

Unfortunately, there is no device that will say, "This job is the best for you." Instead, job seekers have to settle for any method that offers some degree of systematic help.

Such systematic help comes in the form of exploring your pattern of interests. This is one of the factors that contribute to choosing an appropriate occupation and subsequent success in it. For this reason, many researchers have done a great deal of work to assist you in that choice.

One of the research avenues they use comes from finding that people in different jobs have different interests. Next, they ask each person to indicate what he or she likes or dislikes among different work activities, leisure activities, types of people, occupations, and school subjects and then they compare the answers with the interests expressed by successful people in different occupations.

A caution: Merely having similar interests does not say, "This job is the best for you." Many other factors are involved in job happiness and success, among them your personality, intelligence, motivation, experience, and unique abilities.

Another caution: This book cannot present you with an interest scale and provide you with results. You can arrange for this at a local university or other appropriate organization where a trained vocational counselor can help you interpret the results.

A final caution: Knowing and following your interest pattern in choosing a job is more likely related to your happiness in the job than to your success in it. Because of this, it is likely to have some connection with how long you stay there.

Nevertheless, it is probably a good idea, if you have some insight into what interests you, seriously to consider accepting a job that matches your interests and, similarly, to look with a skeptical eye on accepting a job in which your interest is low.

Jobs Can Be Classified

Two of the most prominent researchers into vocational interests are John L. Holland and Edward K. Strong. The latter's earlier research has been continued and updated by David P. Campbell and Jo-Ida Hansen.

These researchers noted some consistent likes and dislikes among people in such jobs as mechanic, farmer, drill press operator, teamster, carpenter, tractor operator, and many others. Such people are generally practical and have good physical or mechanical skills. They enjoy working with their hands and creating things, but not things of an artistic nature. They also tend to be stable, are inclined to be thrifty, enjoy outdoor work, and are better and happier dealing with things than with people. Do you feel you share a good number of these interests and qualities?

Similarly, shared sets of interests have been found among people whose greatest vocational happiness is working in scientific areas. These people, who enjoy analyzing and solving problems, are often creative and innovative in their solutions. They like to work independently, with a minimum of rules. They tend to be orderly, intellectual, and precise, so it is not surprising to find them working as chemists, physicians, and mathematicians and also as laboratory workers, quality control people, and computer analysts, programmers, and technicians. How close does this come to your interests and personal qualities?

Still another group of people who share similar likes and dislikes are those who enjoy the arts. These are just the opposite of the methodical, precise, orderly types just described above. They are, in fact, often disorderly and disorganized. They can be emotional and like to express their emotions. They do so as actors, singers, painters, poets, and dancers. They may also be active in the arts as theater critics or movie reviewers. If they are in advertising, they deal with its artistic side, perhaps as art directors. They may be very imaginative and act on their intuitions, sometimes impulsively. How close to you are these interests and traits?

Still another set of people are "people" people. Unlike farmers and carpenters, who prefer to work with things, and scientists, who prefer to work with ideas, this group prefers to work with people. Hence—no surprise—they are happiest as teachers, social workers, and athletic coaches and trainers. You would expect them to be sociable and they usually are, often accompanying their sociability with tactfulness, kindness, and understanding. These are the people who usually get along well with others and therefore can be quite popular. How well does this description fit you?

Now we come to those folks who enjoy selling or persuading others, who like to use words in these activities and may be good with them, who enjoy the center of attention and even provide leadership.

They regard as important the rewards of their efforts: power and material things. Not unexpectedly, they find success as salespeople and managers, administrators, and business executives. You must have met such people, as they go about their lives and their work with self-confidence, energy, ambition, and, yes, perhaps also with domineering and shoot-from-the-hip tendencies. Can you identify and relate to this description?

Finally, there are the people who enjoy order and structure, such as large organizations provide. They like to have a set of rules to work by, and they follow those rules faithfully as long as they know them. They can be conscientious and fit well into unambiguous situations. They are not interested in being leaders but respond well to leadership by others. Neither are they particularly interested in artistic or physical activities. But give them a clearly defined job and you can depend on them to turn out an orderly, careful piece of work. You usually find them in the business world, where they enjoy jobs like bank teller, bookkeeper, credit manager, tax expert, and some forms of accounting. Does this sound more like you than some of the other groups?

People, Data, and Idea Jobs

Most white-collar jobs can be classified as jobs where "people," "data," or "idea" elements predominate.

People jobs involve large amounts of interpersonal communications. Management jobs are usually classified in this category. Data jobs tend to be administrative in nature and focus on facts and numbers and their analysis. Idea jobs are creative and conceptual in nature. Product and brand managers, for example, have idea jobs.

If you are involved with, or likely to be in white-collar jobs, this next exercise may help you determine which of these three categories is most suitable for you.

The Interests Inventory

A list of thirty-six activities follows. Obtaining an understanding of those you are most interested in is of considerable importance in career planning and job selection, because most people are happiest and do best in those kinds of work in which they have the greatest interest.

On the line to the left of each activity, evaluate your interest according to this code:

- One of my strongest interests. Give this a rating of 1.

- An average interest compared with the others. Give this a rating of 0.

- Not really an interest or no interest at all. Give this a rating of –1.

___ 1. Planning

___ 2. Collecting (information)

___ 3. Setting up budgets

___ 4. Finding correlations and statistical relationships

___ 5. Summarizing (the results of studies)

___ 6. Establishing financial balances

___ 7. Arranging (similar material into categories)

___ 8. Forecasting (sales, expenses)

___ 9. Organizing (committees, work groups, training classes)

___ 10. Collaborating (on a project with others)

___ 11. Questioning (to solve problems or reach conclusions)

___ 12. Auditing (expenses, vendors' invoices)

___ 13. Designing (programs, presentations)

___ 14. Computing

___ 15. Counseling (people problems, work performance)

___ 16. Recommending (courses of action, programs)

___ 17. Connecting (linking ideas from various sources)

___ 18. Categorizing (data into classes)

___ 19. Innovating and inventing

___ 20. Negotiating

___ 21. Researching

___ 22. Selling

___ 23. Administering and managing

___ 24. Writing

___ 25. Serving

___ 26. Coordinating (people's activities)

___ 27. Appraising (people and their performance)

___ 28. Developing (ideas, promotions, strategies, action plans)

___ 29. Problem solving

___ 30. Creating (programs)

___ 31. Consulting

___ 32. Supervising

___ 33. Analyzing

___ 34. Editing

___ 35. Teaching

___ 36. Interpreting

Scoring Your Inventory

Transfer your scores from the inventory to this sheet. Add the numbers in each column and write the total on the line provided. The column with the highest total represents the area of your highest interests. The column with the next highest total represents the area of your second highest interests. The column with the lowest total represents the area of your least interests.

People Occupations	Data Occupations	Idea Occupations
9. _____	2. _____	1. _____
10. _____	3. _____	5. _____
15. _____	4. _____	11. _____
20. _____	6. _____	13. _____
22. _____	7. _____	16. _____
23 _____	8. _____	17. _____
25. _____	12. _____	19. _____
26. _____	14. _____	24. _____
27. _____	18. _____	28. _____
31. _____	21. _____	29. _____
32. _____	33. _____	30. _____
35. _____	34. _____	36. _____
Total: _____	Total: _____	Total: _____

People occupations are those primarily oriented to people: face-to-face contacts involving selling, leading, managing, supervising, helping, and counseling.

Data occupations are those primarily oriented toward data: collecting facts, working with figures, editing numerical and written material, setting up systems, and dealing with details.

Idea occupations are those primarily oriented toward ideas: dealing with abstractions and concepts, developing product programs, creating new approaches.

Summary

Finally, review what you've analyzed about your interest pattern.

1. The strongest area of my interests is the one exhibited by people who enjoy (circle one):

   Physical activities

   Scientific activities

   Artistic activities

   People activities

   Selling and persuading activities

   Orderly and structured activities

2. My weakest area is the one exhibited by people who enjoy (list one from 1): _____

3. I most enjoy activities that are typical of (circle one):

   People occupations

   Data occupations

   Idea occupations

4. I least enjoy activities that are typical of (list one from 1):

   _____

CHAPTER 12

Measure Your Personality

'Twixt the optimist and pessimist
The difference is droll;
The optimist sees the doughnut
But the pessimist sees the hole.

—*McLandburgh Wilson*

IT IS POSSIBLE, IF you are unhappy with your present job, that the dissatisfaction comes from a mismatch between what the job requires and what you do best and are most comfortable with. If your dissatisfaction is associated with difficulties with other people in your workplace, might not this, too, be caused by personality disharmony?

Just as we found groups of people who, in their values, resemble one another and, similarly, we found groups who share interest patterns, so, it turns out, there are groups of people who share similar personality characteristics that are different from other groups.

The analysis of different types of personality is known as *personality typology* and has been a subject for study by philosophers and scholars since ancient times. Hippocrates, usually considered the father of medicine, proposed about 44 B.C.E. that people could be grouped into four main classes: Phlegmatic, or calm (today we might apply the term *unflappable*); choleric, the irritable person; sanguine, the optimist; melancholic, or sad and depressed.

The caution expressed earlier that values and interests only partially contribute to your job success or failure must also be observed with respect to personality. Yet personality is often a major element here, because it is so closely associated with how you get along with your associates, subordinates, and bosses.

It is generally believed that personality develops quite early in childhood. This is because you develop a particular way of interacting with the world that you keep using in talking and acting because you are comfortable with it. It is so characteristic that others perceive this particular style as yours, just as you perceive the styles of others.

These methods of acting and talking become so habitual that sometimes we use them when we don't mean to or want to, even when they can be inappropriate or even harmful. This is especially the case if you are under stress or angry. Thus, not infrequently, the roots of a person's failure in a job lie in misunderstandings or clashes caused by differences in personality.

Since these personality patterns may date back to childhood, it is not surprising that they are difficult to change, and it is unlikely that you can develop a completely different style even in the course of a lifetime.

But you don't really need to. Each personality style has its own characteristics, and no one style is better than another. What is needed is a recognition of the characteristics of that style—in yourself and in others.

The styles we will describe are neither good nor bad; they are simply different. For yourself, you may be able to curb the inappropriate excesses of your style. For others, you may be better able to understand that person's unsuitable behaviors and cope with them more successfully.

But, in fact, understanding the behavior of others is often difficult, even an art. This is because each of us may have a different point of view, a different perspective. Consider this story:

A very wealthy man bought a huge ranch in Arizona and invited some of his closest associates over to see it. After touring some of the 1,500 acres of mountains and rivers and grasslands, he took everybody inside.

The house was as spectacular as the scenery, and behind it was the largest swimming pool anyone had ever seen. However, the gigantic swimming pool was filled with alligators.

The owner explained it this way: "I value courage more than anything else. Courage is what made me a billionaire. In fact, I think courage is such a powerful virtue that if anybody was courageous enough to jump in that pool, swim through those alligators, and make it to the other side, I'd give him anything he wanted—my house, my land, my money."

Of course, everybody laughed at the absurd challenge and had started to follow the owner into the house for lunch when they suddenly heard a splash. Turning around, they saw one guest swimming for his life across the pool, thrashing at the water as the alligators swarmed after him. After several death-defying seconds, the man made it, unharmed, to the other side and pulled himself out.

The wealthy host was absolutely amazed. "You are indeed a man of courage" he said, "and I will stick to my word. What do you want? You can have anything—my house, my land, my money—just name it and it's yours."

The swimmer, breathing heavily, looked up at his host and said, "I just want to know one thing. Who the hell pushed me into that pool?"

To a certain extent, identification of your own personality style can help you identify what kind of job can be a good match or, possibly, what it is about the match between your present job and your personality that may cause problems. By watching others and listening, you can improve your skill in sizing up your own style and theirs.

The Different Types of Personality

A good deal of how we regard personality today stems from the important classification proposed in 1921 by Swiss psychiatrist Carl Gustav Jung, who noted that people have their preferences in the approach they use to go through life.

His theory says that how people behave is consistent and predictable, so much so that when a person exhibits behaviors different from his or her more usual behaviors, others notice this, often with surprise.

Other psychologists have more recently further extended and modified Jung's work. If you choose to read more about personality typology, you will come across such names as Isabel Myers and Katherine Briggs, David Keirsey, and Marilyn Bates, who have developed additional systems.

Several such commonly used systems classify personality into four pairs of types:

1. **Extroverts and Introverts:** This pair deals with how people tend to look at and react to people, objects, the world.
2. **Sensors and Intuitors:** This pair deals with how people tend to gather and perceive information.
3. **Thinkers and Feelers:** This pair deals with how people tend to make decisions. (Be careful with this one. *Thinking* is not connected with intelligence or intellectualism; *feeling* is not connected with emotions; rather, both deal with how decisions are made and the process that is used.)
4. **Judgers and Perceivers:** This pair deals with how people orient to life, what their attitudes are to the outside world.

We will be discussing these pairs, eight types in all, by showing the traits associated with each. But here is a caution: With respect to each pair, people are not either/or but rather more or less.

Every person demonstrates traits associated with both pairs (for example extroverts and introverts) but uses the traits associated with one of the pair more often, is more comfortable with it, and adopts a number of attitudes and ways of thinking associated with that side of the pair.

Thus an individual cannot casually be called an extrovert or an introvert unless, perhaps, he or she is an extreme user of one side of the pair or the other. But an individual can be said to fit closely to a type.

You should try to identify which of the following traits you most commonly use and are most comfortable with. You should also try to identify those traits most characteristic of significant people in your life, including people in your organization: associates, bosses, subordinates. People who tend to favor one side of each pair may not agree with those on the other side, which can, of course, lead to conflicts and misunderstandings.

Your understanding of personality typology can lead to an appreciation of why people react differently to the same conditions or sets of circumstances in your workplace. And, especially by knowing yourself, you may be better able to connect with others on the job and better identify jobs whose requirements are in better harmony with the qualities and traits characteristic of your personality.

Classifying Your Personality

The traits that follow are characteristic of pairs of personality types. See which ones are similar to your own behaviors and preferences and which are not and check YES if like you and NO if not. *Note:* You are likely to find traits similar to your own on both sides of the pairs, but try to identify which side is more typical of you.

Extroverts and Introverts

	Yes	No
• I am outgoing and like to work with people.		
• I react rapidly and meditate about my reaction later.		
• I tend to be action-oriented, am easy to know, and communicate freely with others.		
• I become impatient with slow drawn-out tasks and work that involves few contacts with others.		
• I do less well with jobs that have little change or variety.		
• I am somewhat uncomfortable when required to be independent at work and at decision making.		

How closely does this description include traits that are yours? These feelings fit the type known as extroverts.

	Yes	No
• I do not readily express my feelings and emotions.		
• I like a quiet environment where I can study ideas and reflect and meditate on them.		
• I am careful before I act.		

- I am not happy when I have to act or
  make decisions rapidly, without a good
  deal of thought.   ____   ____

- I dislike noisy, busy environments; I
  dislike being interrupted in my work.   ____   ____

- I dislike work that requires a good deal
  of socializing and communicating.   ____   ____

These qualities are common to introverts. How closely do you present the profile of an introvert, even though you may display some of the qualities of the extrovert?

Sensors and Intuitors

	Yes	No
- I am a pragmatist. Give me the facts, and I'll check to be sure they are true.	____	____
- I trust those facts that are true and remember them.	____	____
- I organize and process the facts.	____	____
- I enjoy work that is detailed; I am patient, orderly, and systematic.	____	____
- I take direction comfortably; I am comfortable and at ease with details, procedures, and rules.	____	____

If you checked the YES column more frequently, you fit the type known as sensors.

	Yes	No
• I enjoy using my imagination and opportunities to be creative.	____	____
• I find problem-solving activities are fun; I like to visualize the future and work on concepts.	____	____
• I am not at all uncomfortable with hunches and solving problems with intuition.	____	____
• I thrive on innovation, complexity, and long-range planning.	____	____
• I don't like stable, routine, repetitive situations and have trouble sitting still unless I am given opportunities to be creative and innovative.	____	____
• I can jump to conclusions and make factual mistakes because of a sixth-sense approach to problems.	____	____

If many of your responses were YES, you have described yourself as an intuitor.

Thinkers and Feelers

	Yes	No
• I evaluate myself as a person who makes careful decisions that are based on logical analytic thinking.	____	____
• I am inclined to be objective, impersonal, and orderly.	____	____

- I stand firm when I reach a decision, based on the principle involved. ____ ____

- I run the risk that, because I stand on principle, others may perceive me as unfeeling, cold, unsympathetic, or insensitive to their feelings, even though they see my decision as being just. ____ ____

Do your responses suggest you may have many of the qualities of a thinker?

	Yes	No

- I tend to stress the need for good interpersonal relationships. ____ ____

- I try to understand other people's needs and viewpoints. ____ ____

- I try, in the presence of disagreements, to negotiate and conciliate and balance the objective decisions of thinkers with empathy. ____ ____

- I do run the risk of going overboard in accepting others' needs and values, thus damaging the quality of my own decisions. ____ ____

- I can become uncomfortable making difficult moves when, for example, as a supervisor, there would be a need for me to discipline or fire a subordinate. ____ ____

Do your responses suggest a match between yourself and people who emphasize other people's feelings?

Judgers and Perceivers

	Yes	No
• I identify with people who approach a problem with a mental set to get a job done with firmness and decisiveness.	___	___
• I start a job with the intention of finishing it and then moving on to the next problem or project.	___	___
• I project self-confidence, certainty, and stick-to-it-iveness until the job is done.	___	___
• I am not at all bothered by deadlines.	___	___
• I may make some impulsive decisions because of a tendency to reach an early judgment of the situation and then close the problem.	___	___
• I like to be prepared for anything that may arise and can, as a result, become upset and bothered by changes in the middle of my dealing with a situation.	___	___
• I can be stubborn and inflexible, impatient with delays or interruptions in getting the work done.	___	___
• I may rush, at times, to get closure without sufficient facts and data.	___	___
• I can be judgmental about other people who interrupt my work.	___	___

Do these traits sound familiar in their resemblance to your own? These are the judgers.

	Yes	No
• I welcome more facts and data.	____	____
• I am not bothered by sudden changes and am always ready for the unexpected.	____	____
• I can see all points of view and even welcome them, since I am flexible.	____	____
• I see myself as "rolling with the punch" and, if given a variety of tasks before any one of them is completed, am perfectly ready to adapt.	____	____
• I sometimes have trouble putting closure to a problem and finishing it.	____	____
• I am not always sure of my decisions or whether I have accumulated enough facts.	____	____
• I am sometimes perceived by others as indecisive and easily distracted.	____	____

How closely do you resemble a perceiver?

Summary

Here are the pairs again currently in regular use as a basis in personality typology:

Extroverts	Introverts
Sensors	Intuitors
Thinkers	Feelers
Judgers	Perceivers

The types whose traits are well suited to jobs in business and industry, particularly in managerial and executive jobs, are listed in the column on the left. A review of the descriptions of these types will reveal people who are practical, concerned with the here-and-now, and eager to get results. These people oppose inefficiency and careless or incomplete processing of problems.

They can be impatient and frustrated with those who are concerned with others' feelings, who keep delaying closure while they collect more facts, whose flexibility interferes with getting the job done. Potentially they can be frustrated, then, at times, by introverts, intuitors, feelers, or perceivers.

Consider your own traits and their implications in terms of vocational career but continue to remember these cautions:

Each of these types has its own strengths and possible weaknesses. And everyone has traits typical of both sides of each pair, but uses the traits of one side more often, is more comfortable with those traits, and tends toward the beliefs and values associated with that side of the pair.

CHAPTER **13**

Measure Your Job Preferences

WE'VE BEEN concentrating on your values, interests, and personality as they relate to career choices. But jobs also have their characteristics. Some involve dealing with many details, others with few. Some involve close supervision, others little. Some are highly structured, with precise ways of doing things; others require free wheeling and spontaneity. Others have clear-cut rules; others are ambiguous. What are your preferences?

On the next page is a list of many important job characteristics. Next to each is a continuum, with five points on the scale. The more to the left your score yourself, the better you feel you deal with the job characteristic listed on the left. The more to the right, the better you deal with the job characteristic on the right.

Fill in a circle to indicate the degree that best describes your preferences. If your circle appears in the middle, it means you don't feel strongly about those characteristics on the left *or* on the right.

After you have responded to all the items, draw a line from top to bottom, connecting all the circles.

Master Job Preference Chart

I Do Best at This						I Do Best at This
Work in office setting	o	o	o	o	●	Work in field
Little travel	o	o	o	o	●	Much travel
More general	●	o	o	o	o	More specific
Not much decision-making responsibility	o	o	o	o	●	Much decision-making responsibility
Little interaction with people outside the company	o	o	o	o	●	Considerable interaction with people outside the company
High technical orientation	o	o	o	o	●	Low technical orientation
High involvement with detail	o	o	o	o	●	Little or no involvement with detail
Management of others	o	o	o	o	●	Little or no management of others
Job structure, rules clear-cut	o	o	o	o	●	Low or no structure. Lots of ambiguity
Line responsibilities	o	o	o	o	●	Staff responsibilities
Flexible working hours	●	o	o	o	o	Fixed working hours
Working with close-knit team	●	o	o	o	o	Little teamwork involved
Work clearly visible to higher management	●	o	o	o	o	Work not easily visible to higher management
High risk, high achievement challenge	o	o	o	o	●	Low risk, low possibility of failure
Close contact with boss	o	o	o	o	●	Little contact with boss
Close contact with others	●	o	o	o	o	Mostly work alone
Work at high pressure/intensity, close deadlines	o	o	o	o	●	Work at slower pace, low pressure, deadlines not close
Work includes unexpected events	o	o	o	o	●	Work predictable, few surprises
Financial rewards based on results	o	o	o	o	●	Financial rewards steady, predictable
Others' work dependent on my work	o	o	o	o	●	Others' work not dependent on my work
Close supervision leads to specific, frequent feedback	o	o	o	o	●	Supervision not close, feedback general, infrequent
Work requires imagination, innovation, creativity	●	o	o	o	o	Little opportunity for imagination, innovation, creativity
Work requires constant thought, take-home work	o	o	o	o	●	Work ends when work day ends
Often requires presentations	o	o	o	o	●	Rarely requires presentations
Lots of report writing	o	o	o	o	●	Relatively little writing required
Work requires organization skills	o	o	o	o	●	Organization skills not important
Many projects go on at same time	●	o	o	o	o	Each project to be completed before next one begins

This gives you a picture of the kind of work you prefer. In the next chapter, you will find preferences charts for a variety of different jobs. You can then compare your chart with these to see the kind of jobs you seem to prefer.

Most important, in evaluating your present job—or any job you are interested in—try to learn the characteristics of those jobs, so as to compare them with your own job preference chart.

PART IV

Identifying Appropriate Jobs

A SHIP'S CAPTAIN on deck one night saw what looked like the lights of another ship coming toward him. He directed his signalman to send the message, "Change your course ten degrees south."

The reply came back: "Change *your* course ten degrees north."

The captain answered, "I am the captain. Change your course south."

The reply: "I am a seaman first class. Change *your* course north."

The infuriated captain signaled back, "Dammit, I say change your course. I am on a battleship."

To which he got this reply: "And I say change *your* course. I am on a lighthouse."

CHAPTER 14

Fifteen Sample Jobs: Finding a Match

Now THAT YOU have completed your job preference chart, you should have developed some insights about the features and characteristics of the kind of work you prefer.

The next step is to compare your preferences with the characteristics of various jobs for which you may qualify, consistent with a good fit with your values, interests, and personality. A good match can represent the difference between job happiness and its absence.

Here's an example of a match that didn't come out quite right. A fellow was once introduced at a meeting as "the most gifted businessman in the country," evidenced by the fact that he had made a million dollars in California oil.

When he rose to speak, he appeared a bit embarrassed. The facts as reported were essentially correct, he said, but he felt compelled to state that it wasn't oil, it was coal; it wasn't California, it was Pennsylvania; and, just to keep the record straight, it wasn't a million, it was a hundred thousand; and it wasn't him, it was his brother; and he didn't make it, he lost it!

Three Types of Jobs

As Chapter 11 made clear, positions in a substantial number of companies may be classified as people jobs, data jobs, and idea jobs. That is the case with the examples of fifteen varied jobs (in a company that manufactures and markets science-based products) that compose the major part of this chapter.

Almost every job, of course, has some people responsibilities, some data aspects, and some opportunities to visualize or use ideas. But by understanding the characteristics of these different types of jobs, you can consider those for which you may be particularly suited.

In those jobs identified as people jobs, the largest portion of time and responsibility involves interacting with others. In data jobs, more time is spent working with numbers, facts, figures, and analysis. In idea jobs, a great deal of time is spent planning, thinking, creating, and finding new ways to do things. A more complete description of each job type follows.

People Occupations

People occupations are those in which the majority of time and effort is spent interacting with others. In a people job, you might speak at length on the telephone, attend and participate in numerous meetings, and meet one-on-one with others formally and informally—impromptu meetings in the hall, for instance—for a large part of the day.

Some of the activities common to these jobs are managing, consulting, counseling, influencing, teaching, negotiating, facilitating, calling, announcing, discussing, and listening. Teamwork is often a theme in people jobs, which could mean that group rewards are more common than individual recognition.

Some of the characteristics exhibited in people jobs are an ability to get along with a wide variety of personalities, well-developed communications skills (both oral and written), a genuine interest in others and in their opinions, and a feeling of satisfaction when sharing and working with others.

Data Occupations

Data occupations are those in which a majority of time and effort is spent working with facts and documents. In a data job you might spend a great deal of time working with a computer, analyzing numbers, identifying trends, seeking facts, or researching a subject. A data person may help others see the reasons behind certain phenomena, such as relevant trends, by interpreting a variety of interconnected data or recommending actions based on the data available. Problem solving and measuring results are often themes in data jobs, which usually means looking for reasons and working with decision makers.

Some of the activities common to data people are analyzing, interpreting, researching, computing, grouping, sorting through facts and data to find relevant ones.

Some of the characteristics data people may exhibit are a systematic approach to their work, the use of logic in problem solving, a respect for accountability, and an ability to search out answers.

Idea Occupations

Idea jobs are those in which a majority of time is spent generating alternatives, finding new ways to do things, and sometimes even finding new things to do.

In an idea job you might spend a great deal of time meeting with others in brainstorming sessions, finding ways to stimulate your own or others' creative juices, following projects and ideas through to completion, and solving problems.

Some of the activities common to an idea job are designing, problem solving, networking, exploring, testing, discussing, trying things out, bouncing ideas around, thinking outside the box, working through the system to get it changed, and creating new systems and processes.

Planning is often a theme in idea jobs, which means looking ahead, predicting fairly accurately what may or may not happen, and deciding what actions need to be taken in either case.

Some of the characteristics idea people may exhibit are creativity, excitement, innovation, interest in the future, ability to see trends early, natural curiosity, and a perhaps childlike ability to see things differently.

Fifteen Occupational Career Charts

Here are the fifteen job examples, arranged under people, data, and idea headings:

People Jobs
Account manager
District manager
Home office human resource
  representative
Sales administrator: meetings
Sales administrator: supplies
Sales recruiter
Sales trainer

Data Jobs
Financial accounting analyst:
  marketing
Financial accounting analyst: sales
Market research analyst
Marketing information services
  analyst

Idea Jobs
Associate product manager
Professional education associate
Professional educational liaison
Science writer

You will notice that many of these jobs are associated with marketing and sales, and some are highly specialized. Their characteristics are described on occupational career charts set up in a manner very similar to your job preference chart.

These charts were completed by people experienced in the designated positions. Keep in mind, however, that each person who holds a job views it in his or her own way. Indeed, the job holder probably puts a personal stamp on the job, changing it in some way by bringing to it individual expertise, knowledge, and skills.

Further, jobs change over time. What you see now could be somewhat different in a year or two. Nevertheless, these charts should give you a fairly good view of the characteristics of these different positions.

Account Manager

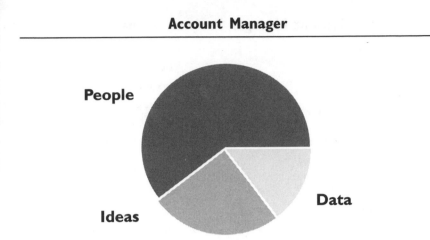

Account Manager: Responsible for applying high-quality, cost-effective selling strategies to major accounts, representing diverse customer bases.

People

- Teaches, trains, and develops telephone sales associates.
- Coordinates sales projects.
- Appraises the performance of telephone sales associates.

Ideas

- Consults with clients.
- Develops and designs projects to be implemented by telephone sales associates.

Data

- Collects sales figures for territory administration.
- Works on budgets.
- Administers salaries.

Account Manager Preference Chart

I Do Best at This						I Do Best at This
Work in office setting	○	●	○	○	○	Work in field
Little travel	○	●	○	○	○	Much travel
More general	○	○	●	○	○	More specific
Not much decision-making responsibility	○	○	○	○	●	Much decision-making responsibility
Little interaction with people outside the company	○	○	○	●	○	Considerable interaction with people outside the company
High technical orientation	●	○	○	○	○	Low technical orientation
High involvement with detail	●	○	○	○	○	Little or no involvement with detail
Management of others	●	○	○	○	○	Little or no management of others
Job structure, rules clear-cut	○	●	○	○	○	Low or no structure. Lots of ambiguity
Line responsibilities	○	○	○	●	○	Staff responsibilities
Flexible working hours	○	○	○	○	●	Fixed working hours
Working with close-knit team	●	○	○	○	○	Little teamwork involved
Work clearly visible to higher management	○	●	○	○	○	Work not easily visible to higher management
High risk, high achievement challenge	○	●	○	○	○	Low risk, low possibility of failure
Close contact with boss	○	●	○	○	○	Little contact with boss
Close contact with others	●	○	○	○	○	Mostly work alone
Work at high pressure/intensity, close deadlines	○	●	○	○	○	Work at slower pace, low pressure, deadlines not close
Work includes unexpected events	●	○	○	○	○	Work predictable, few surprises
Financial rewards based on results	○	○	●	○	○	Financial rewards steady, predictable
Others' work dependent on my work	●	○	○	○	○	Others' work not dependent on my work
Close supervision leads to specific, frequent feedback	○	●	○	○	○	Supervision not close, feedback general, infrequent
Work requires imagination, innovation, creativity	●	○	○	○	○	Little opportunity for imagination, innovation, creativity
Work requires constant thought, take-home work	○	○	●	○	○	Work ends when work day ends
Often requires presentations	●	○	○	○	○	Rarely requires presentations
Lots of report writing	○	●	○	○	○	Relatively little writing required
Work requires organization skills	●	○	○	○	○	Organization skills not important
Many projects go on at same time	●	○	○	○	○	Each project to be completed before next one begins

District Manager

People

Data

Ideas

District Manager: Responsible for the sales representatives assigned to a district as well as for all district activities required to achieve sales goals.

People

- Teaches and trains sales associates

- Appraises the performance of sales associates.

- Counsels sales associates on performance issues and personal opportunities.

- Recruits sales associates

- Coordinates sales functions

- Conducts district meetings.

Ideas

- Creates strategies for the development of individuals and the district as a unit.

- Varies the approach in writing supervisor evaluation letters while making sure there is clear direction and feedback.

- Finds innovative ways to communicate district goals to representatives.

- Establishes plans of action for various areas in a district.

- Plans ways to provide the "motivational environment" for individuals in the district.

Data

- Analyzes district sales call data and district sales dollars.

- Analyzes dollar trends within each territory.

- Audits expenses and other reports.

District Manager Preference Chart

I Do Best at This						I Do Best at This
Work in office setting	○	○	○	○	●	Work in field
Little travel	○	○	●	○	○	Much travel
More general	○	○	○	●	○	More specific
Not much decision-making responsibility	○	○	○	●	○	Much decision-making responsibility
Little interaction with people outside the company	○	○	●	○	○	Considerable interaction with people outside the company
High technical orientation	○	●	○	○	○	Low technical orientation
High involvement with detail	○	●	○	○	○	Little or no involvement with detail
Management of others	●	○	○	○	○	Little or no management of others
Job structure, rules clear-cut	●	○	○	○	○	Low or no structure. Lots of ambiguity
Line responsibilities	●	○	○	○	○	Staff responsibilities
Flexible working hours	○	○	○	○	●	Fixed working hours
Working with close-knit team	●	○	○	○	○	Little teamwork involved
Work clearly visible to higher management	●	○	○	○	○	Work not easily visible to higher management
High risk, high achievement challenge	●	○	○	○	○	Low risk, low possibility of failure
Close contact with boss	○	●	○	○	○	Little contact with boss
Close contact with others	●	○	○	○	○	Mostly work alone
Work at high pressure/intensity, close deadlines	○	●	○	○	○	Work at slower pace, low pressure, deadlines not close
Work includes unexpected events	○	●	○	○	○	Work predictable, few surprises
Financial rewards based on results	●	○	○	○	○	Financial rewards steady, predictable
Others' work dependent on my work	○	○	○	●	○	Others' work not dependent on my work
Close supervision leads to specific, frequent feedback	○	○	●	○	○	Supervision not close, feedback general, infrequent
Work requires imagination, innovation, creativity	○	○	○	●	○	Little opportunity for imagination, innovation, creativity
Work requires constant thought, take-home work	●	○	○	○	○	Work ends when work day ends
Often requires presentations	○	●	○	○	○	Rarely requires presentations
Lots of report writing	○	●	○	○	○	Relatively little writing required
Work requires organization skills	●	○	○	○	○	Organization skills not important
Many projects go on at same time	○	●	○	○	○	Each project to be completed before next one begins

Human Resource Representative—Home Office

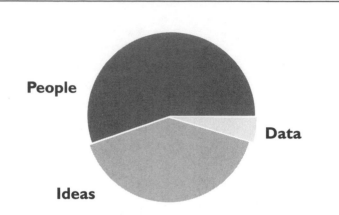

Home Office Human Resource Representative: Responsible for providing home office support for employees of the following types: counseling and problem solving, personnel and organizational development, and compensation and benefits.

People

- Counsels associates on personal and work issues such as job performance.
- Consults with managers to make the best decisions possible.
- Teaches principles and philosophies to home office associates.
- Serves a variety of needs of department members.

Ideas

- Assists managers in developing job descriptions.
- Designs and facilitates group interaction as needed.
- Helps managers find alternative ways to handle issues.

Data

- Works with managers on budgets.

Human Resource Representative— Home Office Preference Chart

I Do Best at This						I Do Best at This
Work in office setting	●	○	○	○	○	Work in field
Little travel	○	●	○	○	○	Much travel
More general	●	○	○	○	○	More specific
Not much decision-making responsibility	○	○	○	○	●	Much decision-making responsibility
Little interaction with people outside the company	○	●	○	○	○	Considerable interaction with people outside the company
High technical orientation	○	○	○	●	○	Low technical orientation
High involvement with detail	○	●	○	○	○	Little or no involvement with detail
Management of others	○	○	○	○	●	Little or no management of others
Job structure, rules clear-cut	○	○	○	○	●	Low or no structure. Lots of ambiguity
Line responsibilities	○	○	○	○	●	Staff responsibilities
Flexible working hours	○	●	○	○	○	Fixed working hours
Working with close-knit team	○	●	○	○	○	Little teamwork involved
Work clearly visible to higher management	●	○	○	○	○	Work not easily visible to higher management
High risk, high achievement challenge	●	○	○	○	○	Low risk, low possibility of failure
Close contact with boss	○	○	●	○	○	Little contact with boss
Close contact with others	●	○	○	○	○	Mostly work alone
Work at high pressure/intensity, close deadlines	●	○	○	○	○	Work at slower pace, low pressure, deadlines not close
Work includes unexpected events	○	●	○	○	○	Work predictable, few surprises
Financial rewards based on results	○	○	●	○	○	Financial rewards steady, predictable
Others' work dependent on my work	○	●	○	○	○	Others' work not dependent on my work
Close supervision leads to specific, frequent feedback	○	○	○	●	○	Supervision not close, feedback general, infrequent
Work requires imagination, innovation, creativity	○	○	○	●	○	Little opportunity for imagination, innovation, creativity
Work requires constant thought, take-home work	○	●	○	○	○	Work ends when work day ends
Often requires presentations	○	●	○	○	○	Rarely requires presentations
Lots of report writing	○	●	○	○	○	Relatively little writing required
Work requires organization skills	●	○	○	○	○	Organization skills not important
Many projects go on at same time	●	○	○	○	○	Each project to be completed before next one begins

Sales Administrator/Meetings

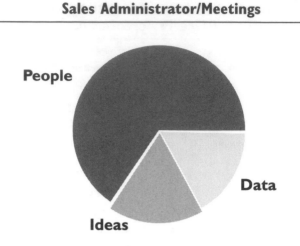

Sales Administrator/Meetings: Responsible for working with individuals at all levels to plan, coordinate, and implement manager, regional, and national meetings.

People

- Collects and responds to feedback from the management team.
- Negotiates meeting contracts with hotels.
- Coordinates sales and marketing programs for manager's meetings.
- Facilitates feedback discussions as they relate to sales and marketing programs.
- Acts as expense report liaison between accounting and sales.

Ideas

- Creates and develops themes for sales and marketing programs.
- Designs meeting format for motivational effect.
- Writes all correspondence related to meetings.

Data

- Forecasts expenses for upcoming meetings.
- Analyzes expenses to meet budget requirements.

Sales Administrator/Meetings Preference Chart

I Do Best at This						I Do Best at This
Work in office setting	○	●	○	○	○	Work in field
Little travel	○	●	○	○	○	Much travel
More general	○	○	○	○	●	More specific
Not much decision-making responsibility	○	○	○	○	●	Much decision-making responsibility
Little interaction with people outside the company	○	○	○	○	●	Considerable interaction with people outside the company
High technical orientation	○	○	●	○	○	Low technical orientation
High involvement with detail	●	○	○	○	○	Little or no involvement with detail
Management of others	○	○	○	○	●	Little or no management of others
Job structure, rules clear-cut	○	○	●	○	○	Low or no structure. Lots of ambiguity
Line responsibilities	○	○	○	○	●	Staff responsibilities
Flexible working hours	○	●	○	○	○	Fixed working hours
Working with close-knit team	●	○	○	○	○	Little teamwork involved
Work clearly visible to higher management	●	○	○	○	○	Work not easily visible to higher management
High risk, high achievement challenge	●	○	○	○	○	Low risk, low possibility of failure
Close contact with boss	●	○	○	○	○	Little contact with boss
Close contact with others	●	○	○	○	○	Mostly work alone
Work at high pressure/intensity, close deadlines	●	○	○	○	○	Work at slower pace, low pressure, deadlines not close
Work includes unexpected events	●	○	○	○	○	Work predictable, few surprises
Financial rewards based on results	○	○	○	●	○	Financial rewards steady, predictable
Others' work dependent on my work	○	●	○	○	○	Others' work not dependent on my work
Close supervision leads to specific, frequent feedback	○	●	○	○	○	Supervision not close, feedback general, infrequent
Work requires imagination, innovation, creativity	●	○	○	○	○	Little opportunity for imagination, innovation, creativity
Work requires constant thought, take-home work	○	●	○	○	○	Work ends when work day ends
Often requires presentations	○	●	○	○	○	Rarely requires presentations
Lots of report writing	○	●	○	○	○	Relatively little writing required
Work requires organization skills	●	○	○	○	○	Organization skills not important
Many projects go on at same time	●	○	○	○	○	Each project to be completed before next one begins

Sales Administrator of Samples & Supplies/ Policies and Procedures

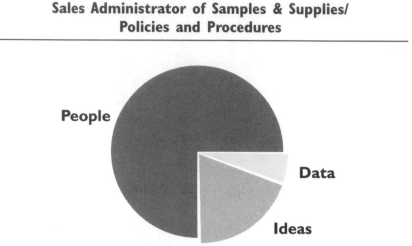

People

Data

Ideas

Sales Administrator/Supplies: Responsible for providing centralized administrative support for sales associates, administering the samples and supplies program, updating and communicating policies and procedures and working on special projects as assigned.

People

- Provides sales support to RM's, DM's, and representatives in terms of samples, supplies, policies, and procedures.
- Administers the samples program.
- Administers the supplies program.
- Sells sales management on ways to improve current programs.

Ideas

- Writes update memos to sales associates.
- Responds to questions and challenges related to sales administration.
- Writes sales section of the policies and procedures manual.

Data

- Analyzes use of sales supplies to maintain optimum inventory levels.

Sales Administrator of Samples & Supplies/ Policies and Procedures Preference Chart

I Do Best at This						I Do Best at This
Work in office setting	●	○	○	○	○	Work in field
Little travel	●	○	○	○	○	Much travel
More general	●	○	○	○	○	More specific
Not much decision-making responsibility	○	●	○	○	○	Much decision-making responsibility
Little interaction with people outside the company	●	○	○	○	○	Considerable interaction with people outside the company
High technical orientation	○	○	○	○	●	Low technical orientation
High involvement with detail	○	○	○	●	○	Little or no involvement with detail
Management of others	○	○	○	●	○	Little or no management of others
Job structure, rules clear-cut	●	○	○	○	○	Low or no structure. Lots of ambiguity
Line responsibilities	○	○	○	○	●	Staff responsibilities
Flexible working hours	○	○	○	○	●	Fixed working hours
Working with close-knit team	●	○	○	○	○	Little teamwork involved
Work clearly visible to higher management	●	○	○	○	○	Work not easily visible to higher management
High risk, high achievement challenge	○	●	○	○	○	Low risk, low possibility of failure
Close contact with boss	●	○	○	○	○	Little contact with boss
Close contact with others	●	○	○	○	○	Mostly work alone
Work at high pressure/intensity, close deadlines	○	●	○	○	○	Work at slower pace, low pressure, deadlines not close
Work includes unexpected events	●	○	○	○	○	Work predictable, few surprises
Financial rewards based on results	○	●	○	○	○	Financial rewards steady, predictable
Others' work dependent on my work	○	●	○	○	○	Others' work not dependent on my work
Close supervision leads to specific, frequent feedback	●	○	○	○	○	Supervision not close, feedback general, infrequent
Work requires imagination, innovation, creativity	○	○	●	○	○	Little opportunity for imagination, innovation, creativity
Work requires constant thought, take-home work	○	○	●	○	○	Work ends when work day ends
Often requires presentations	○	○	●	○	○	Rarely requires presentations
Lots of report writing	○	●	○	○	○	Relatively little writing required
Work requires organization skills	●	○	○	○	○	Organization skills not important
Many projects go on at same time	●	○	○	○	○	Each project to be completed before next one begins

Sales Recruiter

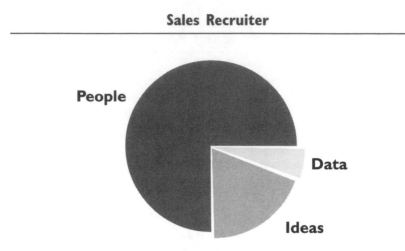

People

Data

Ideas

Sales Recruiter: Responsible for recruiting potential qualified sales associates and referring them to hiring managers. Includes performing candidate searches, background investigations, screening of résumés, and recruiting interviews.

People

- Recruits and interviews people for sales positions.
- Works with field managers in decision-making process of hiring.
- Coordinates recruiting needs/activities with outside agencies, organizations, and colleges.

Ideas

- Provides new approaches to fill a hiring need.
- Reevaluates and implements new recruiting and hiring procedures.

Data

- Provides data related to recruiting/hiring for corporate and government reports.
- Gathers data from interviews, processes that data cognitively, and makes decisions on the "candidacy" of applicants based upon that data.

Sales Recruiter Preference Chart

I Do Best at This						I Do Best at This
Work in office setting	○	○	●	○	○	Work in field
Little travel	○	○	○	●	○	Much travel
More general	○	●	○	○	○	More specific
Not much decision-making responsibility	○	○	○	○	●	Much decision-making responsibility
Little interaction with people outside the company	○	○	○	○	●	Considerable interaction with people outside the company
High technical orientation	○	○	○	●	○	Low technical orientation
High involvement with detail	○	○	●	○	○	Little or no involvement with detail
Management of others	○	○	●	○	○	Little or no management of others
Job structure, rules clear-cut	○	○	●	○	○	Low or no structure. Lots of ambiguity
Line responsibilities	○	○	○	○	●	Staff responsibilities
Flexible working hours	○	○	○	●	○	Fixed working hours
Working with close-knit team	○	○	●	○	○	Little teamwork involved
Work clearly visible to higher management	●	○	○	○	○	Work not easily visible to higher management
High risk, high achievement challenge	○	●	○	○	○	Low risk, low possibility of failure
Close contact with boss	○	○	○	●	○	Little contact with boss
Close contact with others	○	○	●	○	○	Mostly work alone
Work at high pressure/intensity, close deadlines	○	●	○	○	○	Work at slower pace, low pressure, deadlines not close
Work includes unexpected events	○	●	○	○	○	Work predictable, few surprises
Financial rewards based on results	○	○	○	●	○	Financial rewards steady, predictable
Others' work dependent on my work	○	●	○	○	○	Others' work not dependent on my work
Close supervision leads to specific, frequent feedback	○	○	○	○	●	Supervision not close, feedback general, infrequent
Work requires imagination, innovation, creativity	○	○	●	○	○	Little opportunity for imagination, innovation, creativity
Work requires constant thought, take-home work	○	●	○	○	○	Work ends when work day ends
Often requires presentations	○	○	●	○	○	Rarely requires presentations
Lots of report writing	○	○	○	●	○	Relatively little writing required
Work requires organization skills	●	○	○	○	○	Organization skills not important
Many projects go on at same time	●	○	○	○	○	Each project to be completed before next one begins

Sales Trainer

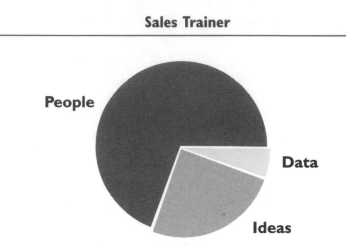

Sales Trainer: Responsible for the home office training of sales representatives and involves coordination of classroom training, writing/updating of training manuals, and classroom teaching.

People

- Organizes training classes for sales associates.
- Appraises sales associates' clinic performance while at sales school.
- Collaborates with marketing and others on projects.
- Administers sales classes.
- Serves the needs of the sales force.

Ideas

- Summarizes the results of studies when putting training materials together.
- Designs presentations for training sales associates.
- Writes correspondence to the sales force.
- Develops selling strategies for six-week programs.
- Connects ideas from many different departments.

Data

- Collects information to be incorporated into lectures and product manuals.

- Researches background information to use when developing training programs.

Sales Trainer Preference Chart

I Do Best at This						I Do Best at This
Work in office setting	●	○	○	○	○	Work in field
Little travel	○	●	○	○	○	Much travel
More general	○	○	○	●	○	More specific
Not much decision-making responsibility	○	●	○	○	○	Much decision-making responsibility
Little interaction with people outside the company	○	●	○	○	○	Considerable interaction with people outside the company
High technical orientation	●	○	○	○	○	Low technical orientation
High involvement with detail	●	○	○	○	○	Little or no involvement with detail
Management of others	○	○	●	○	○	Little or no management of others
Job structure, rules clear-cut	○	●	○	○	○	Low or no structure. Lots of ambiguity
Line responsibilities	○	○	○	○	●	Staff responsibilities
Flexible working hours	○	○	○	○	●	Fixed working hours
Working with close-knit team	○	●	○	○	○	Little teamwork involved
Work clearly visible to higher management	●	○	○	○	○	Work not easily visible to higher management
High risk, high achievement challenge	○	●	○	○	○	Low risk, low possibility of failure
Close contact with boss	●	○	○	○	○	Little contact with boss
Close contact with others	●	○	○	○	○	Mostly work alone
Work at high pressure/intensity, close deadlines	●	○	○	○	○	Work at slower pace, low pressure, deadlines not close
Work includes unexpected events	○	●	○	○	○	Work predictable, few surprises
Financial rewards based on results	○	○	○	○	●	Financial rewards steady, predictable
Others' work dependent on my work	●	○	○	○	○	Others' work not dependent on my work
Close supervision leads to specific, frequent feedback	●	○	○	○	○	Supervision not close, feedback general, infrequent
Work requires imagination, innovation, creativity	●	○	○	○	○	Little opportunity for imagination, innovation, creativity
Work requires constant thought, take-home work	○	○	●	○	○	Work ends when work day ends
Often requires presentations	●	○	○	○	○	Rarely requires presentations
Lots of report writing	●	○	○	○	○	Relatively little writing required
Work requires organization skills	○	●	○	○	○	Organization skills not important
Many projects go on at same time	○	●	○	○	○	Each project to be completed before next one begins

Financial Accounting Analyst—Marketing

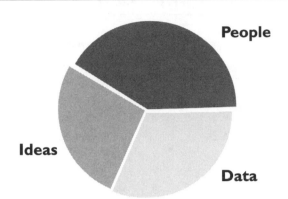

People

Ideas

Data

Financial Accounting Analyst—Marketing: Responsible for counseling and supporting marketing divisions on financial planning and forecasting, including preparation of operating plans, annual profit plans, and related forecasts.

People

- Serves on finance committees and task forces to represent marketing groups.
- Supervises accounting clerks on invoice processing and general administrative duties.
- Helps clients evaluate their financial performance.

Ideas

- Develops one- and three-year profit plans for marketing.
- Recommends allocation of financial resources.
- Develops computer models.

Data

- Sets up budgets and forecasts.
- Audits expenses, vendor invoices, etc.
- Computes and analyzes expense variances compared to financial plans and forecasts.

Financial Accounting Analyst—Marketing Preference Chart

I Do Best at This	1	2	3	4	5	I Do Best at This
Work in office setting	●	○	○	○	○	Work in field
Little travel	○	●	○	○	○	Much travel
More general	○	○	○	●	○	More specific
Not much decision-making responsibility	○	○	●	○	○	Much decision-making responsibility
Little interaction with people outside the company	○	●	○	○	○	Considerable interaction with people outside the company
High technical orientation	○	○	●	○	○	Low technical orientation
High involvement with detail	○	○	●	○	○	Little or no involvement with detail
Management of others	○	○	○	●	○	Little or no management of others
Job structure, rules clear-cut	○	○	●	○	○	Low or no structure. Lots of ambiguity
Line responsibilities	○	○	○	○	●	Staff responsibilities
Flexible working hours	○	○	○	●	○	Fixed working hours
Working with close-knit team	●	○	○	○	○	Little teamwork involved
Work clearly visible to higher management	●	○	○	○	○	Work not easily visible to higher management
High risk, high achievement challenge	○	●	○	○	○	Low risk, low possibility of failure
Close contact with boss	○	●	○	○	○	Little contact with boss
Close contact with others	●	○	○	○	○	Mostly work alone
Work at high pressure/intensity, close deadlines	●	○	○	○	○	Work at slower pace, low pressure, deadlines not close
Work includes unexpected events	○	●	○	○	○	Work predictable, few surprises
Financial rewards based on results	○	○	●	○	○	Financial rewards steady, predictable
Others' work dependent on my work	●	○	○	○	○	Others' work not dependent on my work
Close supervision leads to specific, frequent feedback	○	○	●	○	○	Supervision not close, feedback general, infrequent
Work requires imagination, innovation, creativity	○	○	●	○	○	Little opportunity for imagination, innovation, creativity
Work requires constant thought, take-home work	○	○	●	○	○	Work ends when work day ends
Often requires presentations	●	○	○	○	○	Rarely requires presentations
Lots of report writing	○	○	●	○	○	Relatively little writing required
Work requires organization skills	●	○	○	○	○	Organization skills not important
Many projects go on at same time	●	○	○	○	○	Each project to be completed before next one begins

Financial Accounting Analyst—Sales

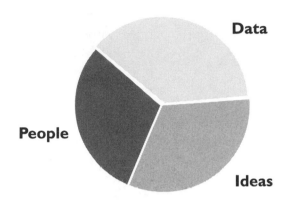

Financial Accounting Analyst—Sales: Responsible for interpreting the needs of sales management, developing and maintaining sales financial performance measurement reports, and directing realignment, quota, and bonus calculation functions.

People

- Coordinates the activities of clerical staff.
- Helps clients evaluate their financial performance.
- Collaborates on quota development.

Ideas

- Develops one- and three-year profit plans for sales.
- Develops computer models for financial performance analysis.
- Recommends and designs potential sales bonus plans.

Data

- Sets up budgets and forecasts for sales.
- Computes and analyzes expense and sales variances to financial plans and quotas.
- Researches and analyzes historical sales and expenses to develop trend analyses.

Financial Accounting Analyst—Sales Preference Chart

I Do Best at This	1	2	3	4	5	I Do Best at This
Work in office setting	○	●	○	○	○	Work in field
Little travel	○	●	○	○	○	Much travel
More general	○	○	○	●	○	More specific
Not much decision-making responsibility	○	○	○	●	○	Much decision-making responsibility
Little interaction with people outside the company	○	○	○	○	●	Considerable interaction with people outside the company
High technical orientation	○	●	○	○	○	Low technical orientation
High involvement with detail	○	●	○	○	○	Little or no involvement with detail
Management of others	○	○	●	○	○	Little or no management of others
Job structure, rules clear-cut	○	●	○	○	○	Low or no structure. Lots of ambiguity
Line responsibilities	○	●	○	○	○	Staff responsibilities
Flexible working hours	○	○	○	○	●	Fixed working hours
Working with close-knit team	○	○	●	○	○	Little teamwork involved
Work clearly visible to higher management	○	●	○	○	○	Work not easily visible to higher management
High risk, high achievement challenge	○	●	○	○	○	Low risk, low possibility of failure
Close contact with boss	○	○	○	●	○	Little contact with boss
Close contact with others	○	●	○	○	○	Mostly work alone
Work at high pressure/intensity, close deadlines	○	●	○	○	○	Work at slower pace, low pressure, deadlines not close
Work includes unexpected events	●	○	○	○	○	Work predictable, few surprises
Financial rewards based on results	○	○	●	○	○	Financial rewards steady, predictable
Others' work dependent on my work	●	○	○	○	○	Others' work not dependent on my work
Close supervision leads to specific, frequent feedback	○	○	○	●	○	Supervision not close, feedback general, infrequent
Work requires imagination, innovation, creativity	○	○	●	○	○	Little opportunity for imagination, innovation, creativity
Work requires constant thought, take-home work	○	●	○	○	○	Work ends when work day ends
Often requires presentations	○	○	●	○	○	Rarely requires presentations
Lots of report writing	○	○	●	○	○	Relatively little writing required
Work requires organization skills	●	○	○	○	○	Organization skills not important
Many projects go on at same time	●	○	○	○	○	Each project to be completed before next one begins

Market Research Analyst

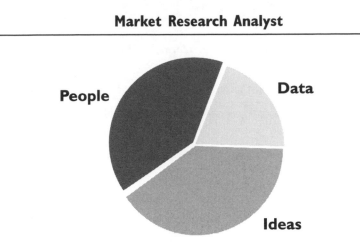

Market Research Analyst: Responsible for conducting market research and providing objective data in current product/market assessments, new product/market assessments, advertising/promotional testing and competitive market forces.

People

- Consults with product management to identify their information needs in support of tactical and strategic decision making.

- Coordinates the efforts of both external (suppliers) and internal groups to implement research studies.

- Serves the research needs of product management.

Ideas

- Designs specific research studies.

- Organizes data into presentations and written reports.

- Recommends courses of action based upon the data.

Data

- Collects, analyzes, and interprets information from primary studies and secondary sources.

- Forecasts product sales and sales of potential new products.

- Uses computers to analyze information, build graphs and tables, etc.

- Finds correlations and statistical relationships.

Market Research Analyst Preference Chart

I Do Best at This	1	2	3	4	5	I Do Best at This
Work in office setting	○	●	○	○	○	Work in field
Little travel	○	●	○	○	○	Much travel
More general	○	○	●	○	○	More specific
Not much decision-making responsibility	○	○	○	●	○	Much decision-making responsibility
Little interaction with people outside the company	○	○	○	●	○	Considerable interaction with people outside the company
High technical orientation	○	●	○	○	○	Low technical orientation
High involvement with detail	●	○	○	○	○	Little or no involvement with detail
Management of others	○	○	○	○	●	Little or no management of others
Job structure, rules clear-cut	○	○	●	○	○	Low or no structure. Lots of ambiguity
Line responsibilities	○	○	○	○	●	Staff responsibilities
Flexible working hours	○	○	○	●	○	Fixed working hours
Working with close-knit team	○	●	○	○	○	Little teamwork involved
Work clearly visible to higher management	●	○	○	○	○	Work not easily visible to higher management
High risk, high achievement challenge	○	●	○	○	○	Low risk, low possibility of failure
Close contact with boss	○	●	○	○	○	Little contact with boss
Close contact with others	○	●	○	○	○	Mostly work alone
Work at high pressure/intensity, close deadlines	○	●	○	○	○	Work at slower pace, low pressure, deadlines not close
Work includes unexpected events	○	●	○	○	○	Work predictable, few surprises
Financial rewards based on results	○	○	○	●	○	Financial rewards steady, predictable
Others' work dependent on my work	○	●	○	○	○	Others' work not dependent on my work
Close supervision leads to specific, frequent feedback	○	●	○	○	○	Supervision not close, feedback general, infrequent
Work requires imagination, innovation, creativity	●	○	○	○	○	Little opportunity for imagination, innovation, creativity
Work requires constant thought, take-home work	○	○	●	○	○	Work ends when work day ends
Often requires presentations	○	○	●	○	○	Rarely requires presentations
Lots of report writing	●	○	○	○	○	Relatively little writing required
Work requires organization skills	●	○	○	○	○	Organization skills not important
Many projects go on at same time	●	○	○	○	○	Each project to be completed before next one begins

Marketing Information Services Analyst

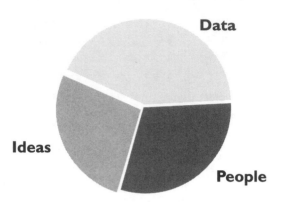

Marketing Information Services Analyst: Responsible for transforming the business needs of sales and marketing into computer system solutions.

People

- Organizes system development project teams.

- Consults with marketing groups to determine their business needs for the purpose of translating this into systems solutions.

- Collaborates with the market research department on various studies.

Ideas

- Designs new system alterations.

- Recommends courses of action to enhance data or get new systems in place.

- Becomes involved in problem-solving involving sales and marketing performance and tracking.

Data

- Analyzes market trends.

- Analyzes and optimizes sales territory realignments.

- Analyzes sales trends and forecasts.

Marketing Information Services Analyst Preference Chart

I Do Best at This						I Do Best at This
Work in office setting	○	●	○	○	○	Work in field
Little travel	○	●	○	○	○	Much travel
More general	○	○	○	○	●	More specific
Not much decision-making responsibility	○	○	○	○	●	Much decision-making responsibility
Little interaction with people outside the company	○	○	○	●	○	Considerable interaction with people outside the company
High technical orientation	○	●	○	○	○	Low technical orientation
High involvement with detail	●	○	○	○	○	Little or no involvement with detail
Management of others	○	○	●	○	○	Little or no management of others
Job structure, rules clear-cut	○	○	○	●	○	Low or no structure. Lots of ambiguity
Line responsibilities	○	○	○	●	○	Staff responsibilities
Flexible working hours	○	○	○	●	○	Fixed working hours
Working with close-knit team	●	○	○	○	○	Little teamwork involved
Work clearly visible to higher management	●	○	○	○	○	Work not easily visible to higher management
High risk, high achievement challenge	●	○	○	○	○	Low risk, low possibility of failure
Close contact with boss	○	●	○	○	○	Little contact with boss
Close contact with others	●	○	○	○	○	Mostly work alone
Work at high pressure/intensity, close deadlines	●	○	○	○	○	Work at slower pace, low pressure, deadlines not close
Work includes unexpected events	●	○	○	○	○	Work predictable, few surprises
Financial rewards based on results	○	○	○	●	○	Financial rewards steady, predictable
Others' work dependent on my work	●	○	○	○	○	Others' work not dependent on my work
Close supervision leads to specific, frequent feedback	○	○	●	○	○	Supervision not close, feedback general, infrequent
Work requires imagination, innovation, creativity	○	●	○	○	○	Little opportunity for imagination, innovation, creativity
Work requires constant thought, take-home work	○	●	○	○	○	Work ends when work day ends
Often requires presentations	○	●	○	○	○	Rarely requires presentations
Lots of report writing	○	○	●	○	○	Relatively little writing required
Work requires organization skills	●	○	○	○	○	Organization skills not important
Many projects go on at same time	●	○	○	○	○	Each project to be completed before next one begins

Associate Product Manager

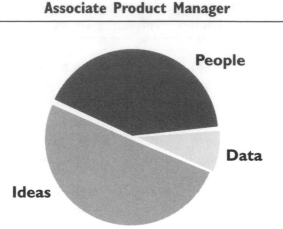

Associate Product Manager: Responsible for assisting the product manager in developing strategies and tactics to meet forecasted budgets, sales, and profit goals.

People

- Collaborates on many projects with others.
- Coordinates people's activities toward achieving marketing goals.
- Consults with the sales force and many other internal groups to get their input and ideas.
- Organizes work groups to meet marketing objectives.

Ideas

- Solves problems that might come up with carrying out marketing plans.
- Plans strategies and tactics based on the input that can be expected from various internal groups.
- Connects ideas and input from a variety of sources and establishes their linkage.

Data

- Sets up marketing budgets and plans.

- Forecasts.

- Collects information from many sources and determines its meaning.

Associate Product Manager Preference Chart

I Do Best at This						I Do Best at This
Work in office setting	○	●	○	○	○	Work in field
Little travel	○	○	●	○	○	Much travel
More general	○	●	○	○	○	More specific
Not much decision-making responsibility	○	○	○	○	●	Much decision-making responsibility
Little interaction with people outside the company	○	○	●	○	○	Considerable interaction with people outside the company
High technical orientation	○	●	○	○	○	Low technical orientation
High involvement with detail	○	○	●	○	○	Little or no involvement with detail
Management of others	○	○	○	○	●	Little or no management of others
Job structure, rules clear-cut	○	○	○	●	○	Low or no structure. Lots of ambiguity
Line responsibilities	○	○	○	○	●	Staff responsibilities
Flexible working hours	○	○	●	○	○	Fixed working hours
Working with close-knit team	●	○	○	○	○	Little teamwork involved
Work clearly visible to higher management	○	●	○	○	○	Work not easily visible to higher management
High risk, high achievement challenge	●	○	○	○	○	Low risk, low possibility of failure
Close contact with boss	○	●	○	○	○	Little contact with boss
Close contact with others	●	○	○	○	○	Mostly work alone
Work at high pressure/intensity, close deadlines	○	●	○	○	○	Work at slower pace, low pressure, deadlines not close
Work includes unexpected events	●	○	○	○	○	Work predictable, few surprises
Financial rewards based on results	○	●	○	○	○	Financial rewards steady, predictable
Others' work dependent on my work	○	●	○	○	○	Others' work not dependent on my work
Close supervision leads to specific, frequent feedback	○	○	●	○	○	Supervision not close, feedback general, infrequent
Work requires imagination, innovation, creativity	○	●	○	○	○	Little opportunity for imagination, innovation, creativity
Work requires constant thought, take-home work	○	●	○	○	○	Work ends when work day ends
Often requires presentations	○	●	○	○	○	Rarely requires presentations
Lots of report writing	○	○	○	●	○	Relatively little writing required
Work requires organization skills	●	○	○	○	○	Organization skills not important
Many projects go on at same time	●	○	○	○	○	Each project to be completed before next one begins

Professional Education Associate

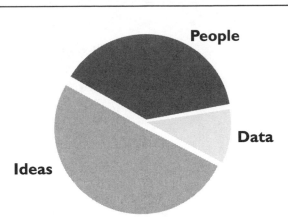

Professional Education Associate: Responsible for planning, organizing and coordinating educational meetings and symposia for the scientific community.

People

- Organizes and coordinates educational programs.
- Collaborates with team members.
- Sells plans for educational programs to management.

Ideas

- Designs plans-of-action to meet program objectives.
- Creates program formats.
- Uses written communications extensively.

Data

- Budgets.
- Researches and analyzes clinical data to be included in program agendas.

Professional Education Associate Preference Chart

I Do Best at This	1	2	3	4	5	I Do Best at This
Work in office setting	○	○	●	○	○	Work in field
Little travel	○	○	○	●	○	Much travel
More general	○	○	○	●	○	More specific
Not much decision-making responsibility	○	○	○	●	○	Much decision-making responsibility
Little interaction with people outside the company	○	○	○	○	●	Considerable interaction with people outside the company
High technical orientation	○	○	●	○	○	Low technical orientation
High involvement with detail	○	●	○	○	○	Little or no involvement with detail
Management of others	○	○	●	○	○	Little or no management of others
Job structure, rules clear-cut	○	○	●	○	○	Low or no structure. Lots of ambiguity
Line responsibilities	○	○	○	○	●	Staff responsibilities
Flexible working hours	○	○	●	○	○	Fixed working hours
Working with close-knit team	○	●	○	○	○	Little teamwork involved
Work clearly visible to higher management	●	○	○	○	○	Work not easily visible to higher management
High risk, high achievement challenge	○	●	○	○	○	Low risk, low possibility of failure
Close contact with boss	○	●	○	○	○	Little contact with boss
Close contact with others	○	●	○	○	○	Mostly work alone
Work at high pressure/intensity, close deadlines	●	○	○	○	○	Work at slower pace, low pressure, deadlines not close
Work includes unexpected events	○	●	○	○	○	Work predictable, few surprises
Financial rewards based on results	○	○	●	○	○	Financial rewards steady, predictable
Others' work dependent on my work	○	●	○	○	○	Others' work not dependent on my work
Close supervision leads to specific, frequent feedback	○	○	●	○	○	Supervision not close, feedback general, infrequent
Work requires imagination, innovation, creativity	○	●	○	○	○	Little opportunity for imagination, innovation, creativity
Work requires constant thought, take-home work	○	●	○	○	○	Work ends when work day ends
Often requires presentations	○	○	●	○	○	Rarely requires presentations
Lots of report writing	○	○	●	○	○	Relatively little writing required
Work requires organization skills	●	○	○	○	○	Organization skills not important
Many projects go on at same time	●	○	○	○	○	Each project to be completed before next one begins

Professional Education Liaison

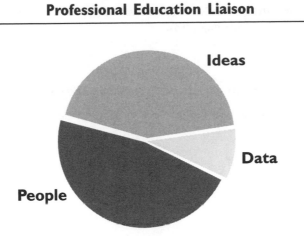

Professional Education Liaison: Responsible for the design and implementation of research and educational programs for scientists in the local community.

People

- Using team approach, both internally and externally, to implement local programs and activities.
- Selling the target audience on the benefits of programs and services.
- Negotiating the implementation of programs to the benefit of all parties involved.
- Coordinating logistics to implement programs.

Ideas

- Questioning potential target audiences about professional needs and opportunities for maximizing program impact, based on local political environment.
- Designing programs and activities to meet identified needs.
- Creating a network within the local community, based on establishing contacts with a variety of sources.

- Utilizing skills of creativity, innovation, and problem solving to accomplish market objectives.

Data

- Collecting information relative to the local marketplace.

- Analyzing educational and research needs of the local community.

Professional Education Liaison Preference Chart

I Do Best at This						I Do Best at This
Work in office setting	O	O	O	O	●	Work in field
Little travel	O	O	O	●	O	Much travel
More general	O	O	●	O	O	More specific
Not much decision-making responsibility	O	O	O	●	O	Much decision-making responsibility
Little interaction with people outside the company	O	O	O	O	●	Considerable interaction with people outside the company
High technical orientation	O	●	O	O	O	Low technical orientation
High involvement with detail	●	O	O	O	O	Little or no involvement with detail
Management of others	O	O	O	O	●	Little or no management of others
Job structure, rules clear-cut	O	●	O	O	O	Low or no structure. Lots of ambiguity
Line responsibilities	O	O	O	●	O	Staff responsibilities
Flexible working hours	O	O	O	●	O	Fixed working hours
Working with close-knit team	●	O	O	O	O	Little teamwork involved
Work clearly visible to higher management	●	O	O	O	O	Work not easily visible to higher management
High risk, high achievement challenge	●	O	O	O	O	Low risk, low possibility of failure
Close contact with boss	O	O	●	O	O	Little contact with boss
Close contact with others	●	O	O	O	O	Mostly work alone
Work at high pressure/intensity, close deadlines	●	O	O	O	O	Work at slower pace, low pressure, deadlines not close
Work includes unexpected events	●	O	O	O	O	Work predictable, few surprises
Financial rewards based on results	O	O	O	O	●	Financial rewards steady, predictable
Others' work dependent on my work	O	O	●	O	O	Others' work not dependent on my work
Close supervision leads to specific, frequent feedback	O	O	O	●	O	Supervision not close, feedback general, infrequent
Work requires imagination, innovation, creativity	●	O	O	O	O	Little opportunity for imagination, innovation, creativity
Work requires constant thought, take-home work	●	O	O	O	O	Work ends when work day ends
Often requires presentations	●	O	O	O	O	Rarely requires presentations
Lots of report writing	O	●	O	O	O	Relatively little writing required
Work requires organization skills	●	O	O	O	O	Organization skills not important
Many projects go on at same time	●	O	O	O	O	Each project to be completed before next one begins

Science Writer

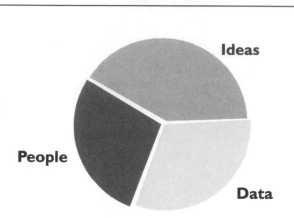

Science Writer: Responsible for preparing written and graphic material for use by various research and development, marketing and sales departments to support the acceptance of the company's products.

People

- Coordinates with authors of books and articles.
- Consults to gain information.
- Collaborates on projects with other internal groups such as marketing and R & R research scientists.

Ideas

- Writes scientific manuscripts, education material, journal articles, etc.
- Plans with marketing groups to determine what types of written material are needed, such as tabloids, journal supplements, and speaker kits.
- Designs presentations for speakers.

Data

- Edits written material.
- Researches subjects before writing.
- Collects information about products in order to write about them.

Science Writer Preference Chart

I Do Best at This	1	2	3	4	5	I Do Best at This
Work in office setting	○	●	○	○	○	Work in field
Little travel	○	●	○	○	○	Much travel
More general	○	○	○	●	○	More specific
Not much decision-making responsibility	○	●	○	○	○	Much decision-making responsibility
Little interaction with people outside the company	○	○	●	○	○	Considerable interaction with people outside the company
High technical orientation	●	○	○	○	○	Low technical orientation
High involvement with detail	●	○	○	○	○	Little or no involvement with detail
Management of others	○	○	●	○	○	Little or no management of others
Job structure, rules clear-cut	○	○	○	○	●	Low or no structure. Lots of ambiguity
Line responsibilities	○	○	○	○	●	Staff responsibilities
Flexible working hours	○	○	●	○	○	Fixed working hours
Working with close-knit team	○	○	●	○	○	Little teamwork involved
Work clearly visible to higher management	●	○	○	○	○	Work not easily visible to higher management
High risk, high achievement challenge	○	○	●	○	○	Low risk, low possibility of failure
Close contact with boss	○	○	○	○	●	Little contact with boss
Close contact with others	○	○	○	○	●	Mostly work alone
Work at high pressure/intensity, close deadlines	○	●	○	○	○	Work at slower pace, low pressure, deadlines not close
Work includes unexpected events	○	●	○	○	○	Work predictable, few surprises
Financial rewards based on results	○	○	○	○	●	Financial rewards steady, predictable
Others' work dependent on my work	○	●	○	○	○	Others' work not dependent on my work
Close supervision leads to specific, frequent feedback	○	○	○	○	●	Supervision not close, feedback general, infrequent
Work requires imagination, innovation, creativity	●	○	○	○	○	Little opportunity for imagination, innovation, creativity
Work requires constant thought, take-home work	○	●	○	○	○	Work ends when work day ends
Often requires presentations	○	○	●	○	○	Rarely requires presentations
Lots of report writing	●	○	○	○	○	Relatively little writing required
Work requires organization skills	●	○	○	○	○	Organization skills not important
Many projects go on at same time	●	○	○	○	○	Each project to be completed before next one begins

Comparing Your Preferences with These Career Charts

If you find it possible to make an acetate or glassine copy of your job preference chart and superimpose it over the occupational career charts, you can immediately see the degree of fit.

You should compare your chart with these fifteen examples to see how close your preferences come to each of them. This will give you some idea of how various positions differ from, or are similar to, your own preferences.

Different Jobs

These fifteen positions are, of course, just a very small sample of the many occupational choices available. There are an estimated five hundred common occupations in the United States. Vocational psychologists typically classify these occupations into six categories:

- **Realistic:** Occupations that are generally described as *robust* and include such jobs as skilled trades and some service and technical occupations.

- **Investigative:** These include scientific and some technical jobs.

- **Artistic:** Artistic, musical, and literary occupations.

- **Social:** Such as teaching and social welfare positions.

- **Enterprising:** Which includes sales and managerial assignments.

- **Conventional:** Here are included clerical and other office positions.

Resources

The Occupational Outlook Handbook, published every two years by the U.S. Bureau of Labor Statistics, is described by that agency as "a nationally recognized source of career information, designed to provide valuable assistance to individuals making decisions about their future work lives." It lists a great variety of jobs within these groups:

Management
Construction
Professional and technical
Production
Sales
Transportation
Administrative support
Laborers and helpers
Service
Mechanics
Job opportunities in the Armed Forces

The 2000–2001 edition lists forty-two industries and, for each, contains information on the nature of the industry, training and advancement, working conditions, earnings and benefits, employment outlook, and occupations in the industry. It also contains lists of organizations that can provide additional information.

You should be able to find a copy in the reference section of your library or obtain your own copy, for a small fee, from the Superintendent of Documents, U.S. Government Printing Office, Washington, D.C. 20402. You can also access its Web site at: http://state.bls.gov and click on the line for the *Occupational Outlook Handbook* (stats.bls.oco)

You may want to use the blank Occupational Career Chart provided here to locate additional career options. Make some copies and see if you can obtain the help of relatives, friends, and neighbors to solicit those people to complete the charts who are working in jobs you suspect would interest you, would be a good fit with your values and personality, and in which you would prosper. Then compare your job preference chart with these examples.

CHAPTER **15**

Being Your Own Boss

For some people, the American dream is to found a small business that becomes successful and possibly grows to become a big business. Others have no desire to become entrepreneurs.

This chapter provides insight into this subject and its relevance (or irrelevance) to you. There are some psychological considerations to be dealt with and also some practical ones.

Psychological Considerations

The chief psychological questions to be considered is: Is being in your own business right for you? Would it be a good fit? No fully usable test to answer this question yet exists but there has been a good deal of research on the subject. One of the principal researchers is David C. McClelland of Harvard.

The Entrepreneur Survey Form

Certain characteristics seem to be associated with successful entrepreneurs. The *Entrepreneur Survey Form* that follows is based on this research and may provide you with useful insights.

Eleven paired statements are presented here, which you are asked to rank in a manner that will reflect your personal feelings, as follow:

- If you fully agree with option A and disagree with B, write 3 on Line A and 0 on Line B. That would be A: 3; B: 0.

- If you fully agree with option B and disagree with A, write 3 on Line B and 0 on Line A, as in A: 0; B: 3.

- If you have some preference for A over B, give a 2 to A and a 1 to B (A: 2; B: 1).

- If you have some preference for B over A, give a 2 to B and a 1 to A (A: 1; B: 2).

Some of the alternatives may seem equally attractive or unattractive. Nevertheless, choose the one that is relatively more acceptable to you.

Do not use any combination of numbers other than those given. A plus B must equal 3.

1. A. I regard work as basically a way to make a living, enabling me to enjoy other aspects of life. __0__
    B. Work, to me, requires a strong the sense of purpose and goals. __3__

2. A. If I were a manager, one of my most important efforts would be to make sure things continued to run smoothly in my department or organization. __2__
    B. If I were a manager, my greatest satisfaction would come from doing a better job, as contrasted to directing my subordinates. __1__

3. A. I most enjoy tasks in which I have a personal responsibility for the outcome. __2__

    B. I believe that luck, politics, and favorable or unfavorable circumstances have the most important influence on one's job success. __1__

4. A. I believe that definite results can come about as a consequence of my activities and decisions. __3__

    B. I believe that no one person can make much of a difference in how an organization or department progresses. __0__

5. A. I feel I deserve some kind of reward for doing a certain task that is assigned to me. __1__

    B. I feel I deserve some kind of reward when the tasks I accomplish get appropriate results. __2__

6. A. In general, I believe there is little one can do to affect important factors in one's surroundings. __1__

    B. I feel my future is basically within my control. __2__

7. A. I prefer to take moderate rather than considerable risks. __1__

    B. I enjoy tackling a very difficult job even when I know the probability is I will fail. __2__

8. A. I consider myself a conservative person and am therefore careful to avoid having to take risks. __0__

    B. To me, a challenge is a task that is neither too easy nor too hard. __3__

9. A. I enjoy taking high risks, as in gambling, with the promise of substantial rewards. __0__

    B. I prefer to take risks when I feel there is a fair chance of succeeding. __3__

10. A. I have a need for fairly quick feedback on how I
am doing. __2__
    B. I am able to be quite patient when waiting for feedback,
even when it is delayed. __1__
11. A. Failure to get feedback on my efforts generally means my
superiors are satisfied with them. __0__
    B. I have a strong desire to get concrete feedback on the
results of my efforts. __3__

Scoring the Survey Form

Make sure that all items have been answered; then enter your points
for the items listed below, and total each column:

Personal Responsibility

Column A		Column B	
1B	3	1A	0
2B	1	2A	2
3A	2	3B	1
4A	3	4B	0
5B	2	5A	1
6B	2	6A	1
Total:	13	Total:	5

Risk Taking

Column A		Column B	
7A	1	7B	2
8B	3	8A	0
9B	3	9A	0
Total:	7	Total:	2

Feedback

Column A	Column B
10A _2_	10B _1_
11B _3_	11A _0_
Total: _5_	Total: _1_

Interpreting the Survey Form

Personal Responsibility. The personal responsibility trait is found in people who see most of the events that occur in their lives as stemming from factors within themselves as opposed to factors outside their control. Research indicates that personal responsibility is associated with entrepreneurs.

People who display personal responsibility believe that their own actions produce outcomes. It has been reported that such people are more alert to new information, more observant, and more curious and are eager to obtain information in order to understand what a situation means. This would make sense for entrepreneurs, who have to acquire as much information as they can and then process the information as quickly as possible.

The greater the score for Column A over Column B, the greater your feeling of personal responsibility.

Risk Taking. A second characteristic of entrepreneurs is reported to be a tendency to set moderate achievement goals and to take calculated risks. If entrepreneurs are too safe and conservative, they may fail to innovate and thus lose out to a bolder competitor. But if they take too many chances, expending too much time, energy, and money, they may incur unacceptable losses.

The greater the difference in the total of the items in Column A over the total in Column B represents the extent to which your answers reflect your degree of risk taking.

Feedback. Successful entrepreneurs are reported to want to know whether they have been successful, and they try to find out. This is the way they get satisfaction from what they have done. This is also why the average business organization provides itself with tables and figures on production and sales costs, profit and loss, and so on.

The greater the difference in the total of the items in Column A over the total in Column B reveals the extent to which your answers point to this desire for concrete and rapid feedback.

A Research-Based Theory

David McClelland asserts that people are motivated by three basic needs: achievement, affiliation, and power. Although everybody has all three needs, different people have them in different degrees.

Achievement is a preeminent need of the entrepreneur, characterized by a need for personal responsibility, taking conservative risks, and setting conservative goals as well as a need for reinforcement that comes from timely feedback.

People with a high need for *affiliation* are primarily concerned with the human side of organizations. They try to maintain harmony and good interpersonal relations. While achievers look for hard facts in the feedback they receive, to verify they are achieving, affiliative persons are focused on receiving approval from their

---

The president of a company underwent a serious operation. While recovering in the hospital, he received the following message from the Board of Directors.

"The Board of Directors met and wish to extend to you their sincere wishes for a speedy recovery. The vote was four to three."

bosses, peers, and subordinates. People whose principal emphasis is on affiliation make decisions based on good people relationships. Such actions are *not* consistent with the kind of decision making associated with entrepreneurship.

People with a strong need for *power* focus neither on good interpersonal relationships nor on achievement. Rather, they consider people as a means to an end and tend to be autocratic in their decision making. This, too, is not consistent with entrepreneurial decision making.

Practical Considerations

About half of all new businesses fail within the first year, so the reasons for such a high failure rate are of paramount concern.

Personal Costs

Especially in the beginning of a new business, a toll is exacted on one's personal life. Would-be entrepreneurs must be able to analyze and evaluate these effects and then ask themselves what they are willing to sacrifice in favor of their business careers.

There needs to be a considerable output in energy. Few entrepreneurs can afford the luxury of a nine-to-five, five-day week. Hardworking employees, who sometimes bemoan their long hours on the job, can be astonished to discover that they need to work even longer and harder in their own businesses.

Changes in lifestyle are frequent. In families with two wage earners, there may be a decision to delay having children until the new business takes off. If a couple decides that both of them should become active in the new business, live-in help may be needed, especially if there are children. Aspiring entrepreneurs must look ahead and make decisions of this kind. In any case, lifestyle changes are inevitable.

Planning and Money

Not only must there be planning regarding home and domestic life, there must be planning for the business as well. In fact, failure to establish a business plan is one of the factors that contribute to the high rate of new-business failures.

Business planning often requires advice and counsel from experienced business and professional people: experts in business management, lawyers, and accountants. Organizations such as the Executive Service Corps are often available to supply such advice and counsel.

While securing advice and counsel can help with planning, for the most part aspiring entrepreneurs should consider entering only those fields for which they have adequate expertise. Lack of experience is a major cause of business failure. Although there are examples of spectacular success in new innovative enterprises, these are the exceptions.

Insufficient capital is most often identified as the cause of new business failures. Aspiring entrepreneurs should probably count on the likelihood that costs will greatly exceed estimates and start a new business only when equipped with sufficient capital.

Readiness to Trade Stability for Growth

There is high comfort level in a stable job. There is less stress, less anxiety, and less personal disruption than in establishing and nurturing a new business. Aspiring entrepreneurs must analyze their willingness to make this trade.

If the new business is unsuccessful, there can be an impact on the previous career. To begin with, time and money can be lost. And returning to one's original career to find a new job equal to the previous one may be difficult.

Timing and Luck

Study the current situation. Is this the time to start a new business? Current economic conditions, the situation in the particular industry, the availability and skills of employees, and other considerations are all important.

Summary

Research suggests that successful entrepreneurs put most emphasis on their personal abilities. There is no question that chance is involved in our lives and career, but successful entrepreneurs seem to feel that for the most part they can make their own luck.

PART V

Getting to Where
You Want to Be

SCHEDULED TO SPEAK at the town hall in a strange city, Bishop Fulton J. Sheen decided to walk from his hotel, even though he was unfamiliar with the route. Sure enough, he became lost and was forced to ask some boys for directions.

One of them asked Sheen, "What are you going to do there?"

"I'm going to give a lecture," replied the bishop.

"About what?"

"On how to get to heaven. Would you like to come along?"

"Are you kidding?" said the boy. "You don't even know how to get to town hall!"

CHAPTER **16**

Establishing Your Goals

THE EXPLORATORY steps you took in previous sections should give you a broad general understanding of where you want to go, what needs you want to meet, and what you want to achieve. Your next step is to establish goals that are more narrowly defined. In doing so, keep in mind the following objectives:

- Finding the realistic options worth pursuing, based on what you have learned so far about who you are and what's out there.

- Discovering whether earlier ideas you may have had about where you want to go are valid, after more mature reflection.

- Increasing your decision-making ability about your career and your future.

- Becoming a stronger candidate for positions to which you aspire by knowing what your abilities are and how to focus on developing them.

- Learning how to pursue your own career planning and to gain support and confirmation by asking the right questions of the right people.

- Focusing not only on the job you want but also on what you want to get out of your life and your work.

A somewhat old-fashioned but still prevailing notion in our society and culture is that somebody who doesn't want to be promoted is an unworthy person. This idea can be strenuously questioned, on the basis that it is a value that cannot and should not be imposed on everybody.

Aside from the question of a person's suitability for promotion, there are uncertainties in all companies and in all industries caused by technological changes, fluctuations in the economy, new influences affecting manufacturing, finance, and marketing, changes in governmental regulations, and other factors.

There are people who can sincerely say, "I like my job and I don't want a promotion or a transfer." It is important that such people be able to say this without feeling guilty nor feel like they are failures; actually, they have made a constructive career decision. Others are equally committed to moving into other areas of their or other organizations upward or laterally.

The Goal Direction Inventory

The inventory that follows may help you in gaining a better understanding of goal directions and options. In completing it, consider your feelings toward your present position or the position you have most recently held.

Try to answer each question candidly, recognizing that no answer is right or wrong, good or bad.

Rate each of the following twenty statements from 1 to 5 by filling in the circle in the appropriate column as indicated.

1 = Strongly disagree (very unlike me)
2 = Disagree (unlike me)
3 = Neither agree nor disagree (neither like nor unlike me)
4 = Agree (like me)
5 = Strongly agree (very much like me)

	1	2	3	4	5
1. I love the work I am doing. I'm becoming a little bored, but I want to stay in the same kind of work.	O	O	O	O	O
2. I'd like to move into another department in my company, though I recognize I don't yet rate an increase in pay or status.	O	O	O	O	O
3. My ambition is to keep moving up to higher jobs in the company.	O	O	O	O	O
4. I can see where my interests, values, and abilities are better met by some position in the company other than where I am, but I'm not sure where.	O	O	O	O	O
5. I need more responsibility than I have now.	O	O	O	O	O
6. My biggest career need right now is to gain new skills and abilities and a broader understanding of this field.	O	O	O	O	O
7. I enjoy my job but require an area more suitably located.	O	O	O	O	O

	1	2	3	4	5

8. I could not be satisfied with a job that lacks supervisory responsibilities.　　○ ○ ○ ○ ○

9. My present job no longer provides me with the challenges I require.　　○ ○ ○ ○ ○

10. I'd like to find out how successful I would be in some other area, but I have only vague ideas where.　　○ ○ ○ ○ ○

11. I would like to gain greater mastery of my current job rather than making a move now.　　○ ○ ○ ○ ○

12. I want to stay in my present kind of work but become more specialized.　　○ ○ ○ ○ ○

13. It's clear to me; I'd like my next move to be into my boss's job.　　○ ○ ○ ○ ○

14. It's time for me to become better at what I do.　　○ ○ ○ ○ ○

15. This book has provided me with theory, but I won't really know what I want until I give some other jobs a try.　　○ ○ ○ ○ ○

16. Gaining experience in other departments is essential for me to accomplish my long-term goals.　　○ ○ ○ ○ ○

17. I probably belong in my present kind of work, but I've identified a different area I'd like to try out.　　○ ○ ○ ○ ○

18. What I want is my boss's job, but the present boss will be in it for

	1	2	3	4	5

quite a while. If I am to move up, I
need to learn about other options.   ○ ○ ○ ○ ○

19. I'm perfectly happy in my job, but I
can see the future. The job is
changing. I want to equip myself to
meet these changes successfully, yet
stay in the same kind of work.   ○ ○ ○ ○ ○

20. I've been identified as a high-
potential person with many possible options. I want to move into
the next area of the company that
is likely to accelerate my advancement, though higher salary and status are not my immediate goals.   ○ ○ ○ ○ ○

Scoring the Inventory

Transfer the number you filled in for each item onto the appropriate blank on this scoring sheet. Then add each column of numbers and write its total in the blank provided.

Job Enrichment

Item No: My Score

1 _____

7 _____

11 _____

14 _____

19 _____

Total: _____

Upward Movement

Item No: My Score

3 _____

5 _____

8 _____

9 _____

13 _____

Total: _____

Job Exploration		Sideways Movement	
Item No: My Score		Item No: My Score	
4	____	2	____
10	____	6	____
15	____	12	____
17	____	16	____
18	____	20	____
Total:	____	Total:	____

Interpreting the Inventory

Let's define these terms and interpret your results.

Job Enrichment. Focusing on job enrichment means remaining in your present job while you use it to provide growth and skill mastery for yourself. It is an appropriate direction if you are seeking to:

- Grow into a specialized position

- Grow in mastery of job skills

- Enlarge the position so as to provide more responsibilities for yourself

- Remain in your present job but change your location so as to better meet vocational or personal needs.

It is also a way to remain productive and grow in ability until other options become available.

Upward Movement. Moving up is the direction for the individual who is looking for enhancement in money, status, and responsibility. There has to be a fit between your interests, values, skills, and abilities and the job's requirements, if you are to be successful and happy. The most sensible approach toward upward movement is to focus on one level or, at most, two levels above your current position and make development plans accordingly.

Job Exploration. Some successful people may have unformed ideas (perhaps no more than dreams) about what else they would like to do, without a clear idea of what that might be.

In terms of career development, this may represent an opportunity for you to move around and try other positions; it may even reinforce the idea that your present work is the best bet. It might also enable you to showcase your abilities and become more visible to colleagues and managers in other departments.

Further, if your scores on two or even all three of the other career directions are about even, it may suggest you consider job exploration.

Sideways Movement. A lateral direction is for people who want to learn new skills and obtain a broader view of the company. It inevitably means meeting new coworkers and often means a new geographical location. It may meet your needs if you are successful in your present position but have abilities that can make you successful in other disciplines as well. It may enlarge your skill and knowledge foundations for further growth in the company. It may or may not provide increased income and status at the entry level.

Summary

As you interpret the results of the Goal Direction Inventory, please carefully consider these questions:

- How difficult will it be for you to prepare for a new goal, taking into account financial, family, and other obligations?

- Which best fits your interests, values, skills, and abilities?

- Which is most in line with opportunities in your present company? In the industry?

- Would your coworkers and/or your supervisor agree with the wisdom of your choice?

- Have you included your family's thinking and needs?

- Will your financial needs be met?

You may want to review your top-rated choices against the realities of these questions.

CHAPTER 17

Validating Your Goals

YOUR GOALS SHOULD be more than good intentions. They need to be properly thought through, well stated, and realistic, and there are criteria by which they may be evaluated.

Criteria

Career goals should be attainable, challenging, timely, specific, and appropriate.

An **attainable** goal is one or at most two levels ahead. It is not realistic to look beyond that because too many unmeasurable variables can intervene. A goal that is attainable is close enough to the level of your abilities that it can be reached by pursuing a realistic number of developmental activities.

The goal should be **challenging**. It should require you to do work that will enlarge your abilities and enhance your self-esteem. And your credentials should compare favorably with coworkers who aspire to the same goal.

Generalized ideas that you want to succeed, or statements that you hope your management will eventually decide what you can do best, are not satisfactory. You need to establish a **timely** plan, expressed specifically in months and years, but not more than three years. You cannot realistically make future plans beyond that. The time frame you state should be realistic also in terms of the developmental activities you wish to complete.

A goal statement should be **specific** and say exactly where you want to be. The acid test is to make sure that any of your coworkers or supervisors who read it would have the same understanding of what you are saying that you do.

The goal should be **appropriate**, in line with what you have discovered about yourself in your self-assessment exercises and what you have discovered you want in your life and work. It should be relevant to your company's or the industry's needs and to the opportunities they can provide.

If your goal direction is self-enrichment, it should state how you would attempt to modify your job.

Other People

There is another way to validate your career development program. It is based on the recognition that others may be equally as able or even better able than you to judge your abilities. Make a list of those people whom you may be able to consult, those who can probably give you intelligent feedback and information about your career development program. They include but are not limited to:

- Your spouse

- A senior family member with business experience

- Your supervisor or manager

- A member of the company's management development or human resources department

- A coworker who is also doing career planning

- A successful business friend or acquaintance

- Someone in the position you aspire to fill

- His or her manager

Edit your list of advisers by asking yourself these questions:

	Yes	No
• Will he or she be able to give me the time I need?	O	O
• Do I interact well with this person?	O	O
• Will such a conversation affect my future relationship with this person favorably, or at least not adversely?	O	O
• Is the timing right from my point of view?	O	O
• Is the timing right from the other person's point of view?	O	O
• Am I ready to respond if he or she asks, "How can I help you?"	O	O
• Are my expectations realistic that this person can help me?	O	O
• Can this person be open and frank with me, in light of his or her position or personal style?	O	O
• Can I ask this person for frankness without being too aggressive and spoiling our relationship?	O	O

Finally, ask yourself if you are properly prepared for this conversation. What do you want as an outcome?

- A validation that the plan is sound?

- An appraisal that your choice of career options is a good match with your abilities?

- A more realistic reworking of your program?

- An appraisal of whether your program is in harmony with your family and their needs?

- Advice on other resources that may be available in career planning?

CHAPTER **18**

Developing the Needed Skills and Abilities

You can observe a lot by watching.

—*Yogi Berra*

GOALS ARE ACHIEVED by developing the tools for reaching success in your career. First, you should identify those skills and abilities you need for the goals you have chosen. To remain realistic, you should choose no more than four developmental areas. Then you should consider the action steps you need to undertake. Action steps are the learning and developmental activities that are the link between where you are and where you want to be.

Skills and Abilities to Develop or Sharpen:

1. _____

2. _____

3. _____

4. _____

Action Steps to Pursue:

1. _____

2. _____

3. _____

4. _____

Completion Date: _____

Ways to Measure My Progress:

1. _____

2. _____

3. _____

4. _____

General Developmental Activities

In addition there are certain activities you can resolve to do that can broaden your knowledge, overcome learning gaps, and strengthen your skills. The most important are:

1. **Observing:** This activity is especially important because it is the basis of modeling the behavior of others. Much of

our adult activity stems from observations we made in childhood. Through observing, we can replicate those behaviors of others which we admire and of which we approve.

2. **Listening:** This is similar to observing. In addition, audio-cassette tapes are available for self-directed learning, for busy people who can listen while driving and in free time.

3. **Reading:** There are many self-directed learning courses in the form of books and booklets, correspondence courses, and online instruction.

4. **Consulting:** People you encounter within and outside your company, and people in departments other than your own, can expand your base of knowledge.

5. **Testing:** An approach to new ways of accomplishing things by testing new ideas and procedures can bring out useful, visible achievements on the job.

Testing can also contribute to your ability to do inventive and innovative thinking. It is especially useful if your goal direction is job enrichment.

Specific Developmental Activities

In addition to the general activities you can plan to undertake, here is a list of specific activities that can go into your developmental program:

1. Ask your supervisor or manager if he or she can provide on-the-job coaching and developmental counseling.

2. Keep alert to opportunities to create job-enrichment activities.

3. See if you can be assigned to the project team, task force, or other special assignments that may exist in your company.

4. Enroll in appropriate technical school, college, or university courses.
5. Investigate and enroll in appropriate online (distance learning) courses.
6. Serve as instructor or trainer, especially of new employees in your department.
7. If appropriate, take advantage of opportunities to become involved in making presentations and participating in meetings.
8. Obtain information and counsel from people in the organization who specialize in areas in which you are interested.
9. Study manuals, bulletins, reports, and other printed material published by your organization or others in the industry.
10. Do planned reading in relevant specialized fields, such as technical books, magazines and journals, and industry publications.
11. Join and participate in technical and professional societies as appropriate.
12. Do planned reading in general business areas, such as finance, marketing, manufacturing, research, and management.
13. Actively participate in community and civic affairs.
14. Attend selected conferences, lectures, workshops, panels, or seminars.

PART SIX

Finding a Job That Fits

ONE DAY A sign appeared in an office window: *Help wanted. Must type 70 words a minute. Must be computer literate. Must be bilingual. An equal opportunity employer.*

A dog ambling down the street saw the sign, walked in, and applied for the job. The office manager said, "I can't hire a dog for this job."

The dog pointed to the line: *An equal opportunity employer.* The manager said, "Take this letter and type it."

The dog went off to the typewriter and returned minutes later with the finished letter, perfectly typed. So the manager said, "Here's a problem. Write a computer program for it and run it." Fifteen minutes later, the dog came back with the correct answer.

The manager still wasn't convinced. "I can't hire a dog for this position," he said. "You've got to be bilingual." The dog looked up at the manager and said, "Meow."

CHAPTER **19**

Preparing to Get Fired

The business cycle is no cycle for sport.
It's not for the leather-jacketed sort.
It's not for the scarf, it's not for the boot:
I ride the thing in a business suit.

—Richard Armour

UNTIL THE BUSINESS cycle is repealed, we can confidently expect that periods of high employment will be followed by downsizings and layoffs, followed by an upswing in employment once again. Throughout, there will be individual terminations and individual resignations.

For this reason, preparation for all these contingencies is crucial. The impact of terminations can be severe, both financially and psychologically.

How to Spot Signs of a Layoff

You are unlikely to be told directly that one of these days you will be fired. Consider the advice Sky Masterson was given by his father. (Sky was the hero of the story *The Idyll of Miss Sarah Brown* by Damon Runyon, which became the hit musical *Guys and Dolls*.)

"Some day, somewhere, a guy is going to come to you and show you a nice brand-new deck of cards on which the seal is never broken, and this guy is going to offer to bet you that the Jack of Spades will jump out of this deck and squirt cider in your ear. But son, do not bet him, for as sure as you do, you are going to get an ear full of cider."

In spite of reassurances that your job is safe, if you have any suspicion to the contrary, be prepared so you don't get an ear full of cider. Always be alert to the possibility of downsizing, even though you have no clear evidence that it is about to happen. You might be able to deflect the ax so it doesn't fall on you. You might be able, through preparation, to lubricate your efforts to secure a new job. And you might be able to lessen the psychological consequences.

When you suspect downsizing may be on its way, raise your antennae and look for clues in what's happening around you.

- The executives who customarily manage by "walking around" are hibernating, or they may be in private meetings that occur with unaccustomed frequency.

- Normal vacancies caused by people leaving or retiring are not being filled, which is abnormal.

- To adjust to the unfilled vacancies, departments are being reorganized.

- Controls on spending are being tightened.

- Projects are being halted in midstream or suspended indefinitely.

- Orders have quit coming in.

- Customers are quiet, perhaps lost.

- Payments for expenses are late, and there are other signs of cash-flow problems.

Your fears seem about to be realized. What do you need to do?

- Make copies of your important personnel and other papers—401K reports, compensation and bonus records, and performance appraisals—and take them home.

- Print out business and personal phone numbers, e-mail addresses, and important Web sites from your computer or copy them on a floppy disk.

- Keep up to date with what your coworkers find out. Trading information with them can enhance your understanding of what is going on.

- Start actively searching trade papers, newsletters, newspapers, magazines, and journals for reports about your company, its competitors, and the industry in general.

- Stay in close contact with the boss. Make sure he or she knows how hard you are working. Showcase what you are doing: do extra work; stay a little later.

- Keep on good terms with everyone: your boss, coworkers, customers. The payoff may come later.

- Keep an eye out for new opportunities, not necessarily in the same industry. Since the ax may fall at any time and since the company doesn't commit itself to lifetime employment, act accordingly. Your loyalty is to yourself.

- Update your résumé and be ready to tailor it to different possible job opportunities. If you are not familiar with how to write an effective résumé, free

help is readily available at these Web sites:
www.jobweb.com, www.Headhunter.net, and
www.jobstar.org. You can find books and handbooks
at www.amazon.com and www.barnesandnoble.com.

- Pretend you are about to have your first interview.
Rehearse your oral presentation. Role-play an interview
with your spouse, other relatives, or a friend. Equip
them with questions, especially the tough ones, you
think an interviewer would be likely to ask.

- Find out your company's termination rules. Make
friends with people in human resources or personnel.
They can provide information about layoff policies and
appropriate local and community resources.

Departure Do's and Don'ts

Understandably, your immediate reaction may be bitterness, even
hostility. Your feelings of self-worth have been badly bruised. Most
important: Don't resign (you may lose all your benefits) and do protect your reputation by blocking any negative responses, such as
threatening to sue or quit.

Do avoid signing any company offer that day. Ask for the offer
in writing. Tell the company you need time to think it over, and
schedule a follow-up meeting. If you are age forty and over, U.S. law
requires your employer to give you twenty-one days (forty-five days
in the case of a mass layoff) to consider the offer before signing a
release or a waiver.

Remain polite and mature in asking when you can pick up your
belongings so as to avoid the embarrassing experience of packing
up your stuff with everyone watching. Find out if you can check
your voice mail and whether the company is willing to forward your
e-mail. Make sure you have a personal, not company, e-mail address.

Read the company's handbook to review whether the package
offered contains the promised benefits, and check with other laid-
off employees to compare your offer with theirs.

Now you are ready for the scheduled follow-up meeting. A generally used rule of thumb is that it will take at least a month for every $10,000 a year an employee earns to find an appropriate job. For this reason, the dollar severance and outplacement services in the package are especially valuable.

Severance Pay

A pretty typical severance offer is two to three weeks' salary for each year you've been with the company. Ask for one month per year when you start negotiating.

Medical Benefits

The health plan is, of course, very important to you. Start negotiating by asking to be kept on the company's health plan for a year. For the company, keeping you enrolled is less expensive than the severance payment. Still, you may have to settle for three or six months. Keep in mind that a federal law, COBRA, gives you the right to continue health coverage at your own expense.

Other Benefits

There are additional possible benefits you may be owed, such as unused vacation time, and what you are entitled to should be set forth in writing. You may be owed a prorated amount of the year-end bonus, if your company has one. Try to get the best deal you can if you are close to being vested in a pension or stock-option plan.

References

Negotiate the reference you will receive and secure it in writing. Get in touch with those people who will provide references. Thank them and indicate to them the strengths and assets you plan to emphasize in your contacts with prospective employers. If you cannot secure references you consider favorable, ask your supervisor or the human resource department simply to give your dates of employment and job title to a prospective employer.

Resources

The following Internet resources are available to you:

Equal Employment Opportunity Commission: www.eeoc.gov

Fortney & Klingshirm: www.myemploymentlawyer.com

Information and advice from employment lawyers.

www.NOLO.com and www.nolopress.com

Describes rights of employees losing or leaving a job.

U.S. Department of Labor: www.dol.gov

Information on unemployment benefits and health insurance under COBRA

After the Ax Has Fallen

First of all, develop and maintain a positive mental attitude. Don't panic; especially, don't sound panicked. Don't sound angry or needy. Otherwise, you run the risk of dissipating your energy and developing a posture of chronic anger and anxiety. Besides everything else, this can result in poor performance at interviews.

Most experts suggest you avoid being in a hurry to interview, if that is at all possible or practical. You are likely to present yourself much more successfully when the hurt and the anger have died down. Settle down and, if possible, wait a week or two. Consider carefully the chapters in Part I on how to evaluate a job and the chapters in Part IV on self-assessment. They will help you formulate plans and ideas on the companies you may be interested in, your short- and long-term career goals, and the companies located near enough to you geographically that may be potential employers.

From your human resources or personnel department you will need:

- Your employment record, to help in registering for unemployment benefits.

- Information on the assistance the company will provide to help you obtain reemployment.

- A letter of recommendation. It may be helpful; at the least it may bolster your ego and self-confidence.

Obtain the separation data in writing. If the financial package is substantial, consider having a lawyer review it.

Start to network. Send out e-mails and letters and make phone calls to everybody you think may be able to help. This can include friends, business associates, customers, and others outside the company with whom you have had successful contact. Tell them you are ready to accept new challenges. Tell them how to reach you by mail or phone but make it clear that you do not expect a reply unless they have useful information for you. Do not sound angry, self-pitying, or hostile to your past employer. Try to take a long-term view. Sooner or later you'll get another job and feel better.

This may be your chance to get out of a rut and consider various career options. Sit down with your spouse and make plans: How long will it take to find a new job? Overestimate the time, to be on the safe side. Based on this, and taking into account whatever other income may be coming in, draw up a new budget to follow. What expenditures will have to be discontinued? Which ones must be maintained? What extra efforts need to be made by your spouse and the children?

Manage the psychological effects: Don't take out your hurt and anger on the family or do foolish things to yourself like drinking or smoking or using drugs. Instead, get rid of the pain and rage in some harmless activity, like working out. Talk about your feelings to others, especially with good listeners who are supportive and understanding. This is most important and is the kind of therapy that is the basis of psychological therapy. Don't talk about your feelings over the dinner table, with the kids present. Instead, arrange a time for updating your spouse, and then quit talking about it at home for the balance of the day.

Unless you are a recent college graduate, you may be eligible for some tax breaks. Save your receipts, employment agency fees, bills for résumé writing and typing services, printing and mailing costs, fees for want ads, phone calls, and travel expenses. Your expenses must amount to more than 2 percent of your adjusted gross income, and your search must be for a job in the same field where you worked in the past. Also, you must be able to show that your search has been continuous, without a substantial period of time between your last job and your hunt for a new one.

CHAPTER 20

Where to Look for Openings

THERE IS NO single best source, agency, or organization to use in searching for a job. Based on their histories and experiences, employers use differing sources. Sometimes the sources for available jobs that are best one year are not so good the next, such as the employment agency that may have functioned well for you at one time but then proceeds to go downhill when its personnel and maybe even its ownership change. Also changed will be its relationships with employers who may have available positions to list.

Companies train their recruiters to try to collect as many applicants as possible. Their concept is that the more applicants they have in the pool, the more likely they are to find a greater number of qualified people.

You should operate on the same reasoning. The more job openings you can pursue, the better your chances of finding the one that is a good fit for you. And the more sources you use, the more job offers you are likely to collect. Your motto should be "Leave no stone unturned."

Conventional Job Sources

Employment Agencies

Of first importance here is the matter of ethics and reliability: Most employment agencies are licensed. If you have a question about this, you can check with your state employment office (now called in some states a one-stop career center). Another way to judge an agency's ethics and reliability is to find out if they are members of the National Association of Personnel Services, or NAPS (3133 Mount Vernon Avenue, Alexandria, VA: www.napsweb.org, (703) 684-0180). This association requires adherence to a code of ethics if a member agency is to maintain membership. Otherwise, there are few rules regarding how to choose and work with an agency. Find out who pays the fee—usually the employer but sometimes the applicant when placed in a job.

Look first for agencies that specialize in certain types of jobs if this is appropriate and relevant to your qualifications. Big ads with many listings generally suggest the agency is larger, older, and possibly has more jobs to fill. A visit to the agency and a look around the premises should also give you some idea of the agency's stability and reliability.

A reliable agency should be able to provide you with most or all of the following information about an employer it represents:

1. Company information: the company's full name, address, whether it is a division or parent company, the type of business, and its size
2. Information about the job: title of the position, duties (including functions) to be performed, supervisory responsibility if any, makeup of a typical day
3. Location of the job and its hours
4. Status with the company: salary range, commission, or bonus
5. Applicant requirements: necessary skills, physical requirements if appropriate, and a statement that the company is an equal opportunity employer

6. What the company offers: salary progression plan, advancement potential, health benefits, and vacation and leave policies
7. Payment of the agency fee (employer or applicant)
8. Information regarding interview: name and phone number of person to contact, any other person to contact, and location and hours for the interview

One-Stop Career Centers

These are the successors to the state employment offices of yesteryear and deserve your attention. They have come about principally because of the 1998 Workforce Investment Act, a federal law that requires states to give all residents access to a wide variety of training, employment, and educational services at a single neighborhood location. Not all states have fully adopted these changes, but they are expected to do so by the year 2006.

The offices help both unemployed and working people who are looking for advanced training and new careers. They offer job counseling and recruitment, computer training, free faxing, Internet access, and workshops on résumé writing, interviewing, and starting a small business. They provide job search assistance and information on labor trends.

In most states, it is no longer necessary to show up in person each week to secure unemployment benefits and to affirm that you are still unemployed. Instead, if you are unemployed, you can access a computerized system that allows the retrieval of tax records and the authorization of benefit checks to be mailed. One visit is usually required to watch a five-minute video orientation that explains the agency's services.

Newspapers

Newspapers list jobs in two formats. First are the classified ads. The downside here is that, unless you have highly specialized skills, you will find yourself in competition with a great many applicants, thus reducing your chances considerably.

Second are the display ads. You generally find these in the financial section and sometimes in the sports section of the newspaper. Your chances are better here if you can qualify, because the jobs being advertised are generally more specialized.

As you examine both types of ads, you will find some with no mention of the employer. These are called blind ads, inserted in this way to avoid alerting the company's own employees to the ad's appearance.

You also need to be aware that, for some reason, certain days are better than others for job listings. This varies from city to city, but Sunday is best nearly everywhere.

Trade Papers, Magazines, and Newsletters

While a few periodicals list classified ads, mostly they carry display ads. But keep in mind that an ad that appears in January was probably inserted in November. Hence, these publications are usually used by employers for specialized or technical jobs, where the supply of qualified people is limited.

Colleges, Technical, and Professional Schools

Nearly all educational organizations have placement services to aid students, graduates, and employers. If you are a graduate or former student, it is important to stay in touch with the person heading up the placement service. It may be even more important to stay in touch with, and cultivate, influential professors and instructors; recruiters and employment managers are in contact with them. Remember the adage "Out of sight, out of mind," and keep your contacts frequent and current.

Online Job Sources

Computerized offerings tend to focus on specific types of jobs, or specific areas of the country, but are becoming good sources for jobs in general. Here are some examples:

- www.hotjobs.com: You can cut and paste your résumé on this well-organized site.

- www.monster.com: You can directly contact the company that lists its openings here, but the lists are long, so using this worthwhile site can be tedious.

- www.mediabistro.com: This puts you in touch with jobs in print and news media, often in the New York area. Most jobs listed are entry level, but there are some senior-level editorial jobs.

- www.journalismjobs.com: Just the reverse of the foregoing, this lists jobs available on small-town newspapers and is national in scope.

- www.craigslist.com: This Web site is principally technology oriented, focused on the Bay area of California, but it is expanding nationally, both geographically and in the types of jobs available.

- www.firsttuesday.com: This site concentrates on start-up companies looking for younger employees.

- www.headhunter.net. As the name suggests, mostly high-paying jobs are listed here.

- www.thestandard.com/jobs: These are also high-level jobs, mostly placed by executive search firms.

Other Job Sources

Executive Search Firms

These agencies, commonly called headhunters, choose areas of specialization, such as sales, computer specialists, and certain types of engineering. They usually deal with jobs higher than entry level.

Big Corporations

These firms, among them Sun Microsystems and Nortel, have their own recruiting sites. Access their home page and then click on the recruiting link.

Networking

Many employment experts agree that the best and most fruitful of all job sources is networking, the individual and group exchange of information.

Young Job Seekers

With little experience and few contacts, young job seekers are less likely to be successful at networking. They must do their job-seeking homework especially conscientiously. If you are a young job seeker, you need to study prospective employers closely, focusing on companies that are actually hiring. Also, start searching the help-wanted pages of newspapers and magazines and the job listings on the Internet, even while you are collecting unemployment insurance.

Of course, even the most generous weekly unemployment benefits are less than half an employee's previous compensation.

Here are the states with the most generous benefits. The figures, from the Economic Policy Institute, are for a worker with two children and an employed wife in 2001.

State	Maximum Benefits	Percent of Income Replaced for Average Worker
Massachusetts	$527	36%
Washington	$441	40%
Pennsylvania	$438	40%
Rhode Island	$437	41%
New Jersey	$429	35%
Connecticut	$427	27%
Minnesota	$427	43%
New York	$405	29%
Illinois	$392	35%
Oregon	$376	38%

If you can possibly do so, avoid accepting a job you would be unhappy in. Try to hold out. Collect unemployment insurance a little longer and wait for an opportunity you really like.

Older Job Seeker

The late Governor Lawton Chiles, a native Floridian with deep roots in the state's rural past, often larded his speech with old folk sayings. He would say, when talking about hunting raccoons, which are nocturnal animals, "The old he 'coon walks just before the light of day."

The he 'coon is the biggest, craftiest raccoon. The younger, less experienced raccoons go out early, but the he 'coon knows to wait until almost dawn, when the hunting dogs are tired, before venturing out.

To apply that to finding a job, the less experienced hunters go out early to employment agencies, newspapers, advertisements, and state career centers. This is understandable. But the relationships you have established in your past employment can be tapped for possible help and are likely to be the best source of productive leads. It is likely you can best contact those people in the evening, when they are relaxed and free to talk with you.

Go after suppliers you dealt with, who visit different firms, often in the same industry. They are likely to be aware of present or near-term future job openings. The same is true of your last employer's customers. It is worthwhile, also, to keep in touch with your former coworkers. And it is very important to continue to attend trade meetings and conventions if at all possible. Companies often send managers and recruiters to these meetings, precisely to look for future employees.

CHAPTER **21**

The Hiring Process: First Steps

MOST GOOD-SIZED well-organized companies have established hiring systems that follow an established procedure. If you understand how this works, you will be prepared to deal with it.

First, they develop a description of the job. Based on the job description, they establish a list of qualifications (these can also be referred to as *dimensions, competencies, characteristics,* or *skills*) required by applicants if they are to perform the job duties and responsibilities successfully.

Next, they use various recruiting methods and sources to find applicants. Usually they try to collect a substantial number of applicants, so as to provide the largest choice. An exception occurs when the job involves specialized skills and available applicants are few.

At this point, the selection process begins in the form of a series of steps. First, a preliminary screening is conducted. This may involve the discarding of résumés that show the applicant lacks the necessary qualifications. A brief interview or a telephone interview may be conducted for the same purpose.

If the necessary qualifications seem to be present, the applicant is asked to complete the company's application form, which is then further screened.

Next, if the company is still interested, the applicant is asked to appear for a much more thorough interview.

Finally if the applicant passes this depth interview, the company checks work references. It may also perform a credit check and ask the applicant to undergo a medical examination. Passing some sort of selection test may also be required.

The first step, preliminary screening, is covered in this chapter, with special attention to preparing your résumé, as is the second step, filling out the application form. Discussion of the depth interview appears in Chapters 22 and 23, and the final steps make up Chapter 24.

But first, a word about legal considerations. The U.S. government, most states, and even some cities and counties have laws dealing with employment discrimination and affirmative action. While these laws and their interpretation are complex, you should be aware of the following as you go through the hiring process:

- The hiring system must measure the characteristics or skills that are needed for successful job performance. And only entry-level characteristics and skills can be required if the job is at entry level.

- Every step in the hiring process must also deal with job-related skills and characteristics. If is doesn't, it cannot be used.

- The system must be used uniformly with all applicants in a particular job category.

- Certain states, cities, and counties have some additional regulations.

Most people involved in hiring understand these rules and observe them. If they do not, it is possible they may not intend to violate the law and discriminate, although the law is not based on intent. You will need to decide whether to call attention to failure to observe the law, unless the violations are flagrant and intended to discriminate.

Preliminary Screening

As a first step, companies use preliminary screening to find promising candidates and to avoid wasting time with poor prospects. This, of course, results in saving time for the job applicant as well.

The aim of all preliminary screening is to determine whether the applicant meets the basic job requirements in education, experience, skills, and characteristics, so that he or she can be considered further. Preliminary screening can be of three types: by résumé, telephone, and interview.

The Résumé

Since saving time is the employer's principal motivation (and since he or she may very well be inundated with letters), chances are your résumé will get one quick scan. Unless you succeed in hooking the reader in that moment or two, your letter will land in the reject pile, along with your hopes for that job.

For this reason, although the résumé is a brief document used at the very beginning of the hiring process, preparing your résumé is so important that we will spend half this chapter on helping you to do it properly.

The purpose of the résumé is simple. It is to get you to the next step, an application form or an interview in depth. The résumé is usually the first contact an employer has with you. It had better be a good sales document.

There are three types of résumés: chronological, functional, and combination.

- Chronological: This gives employment history in reverse chronological order, last job first. This is the form to use if you have an employment history relevant to the contemplated position and your history is good, with no gaps.

- Functional: This lists skills, background, and achievements but doesn't include employment dates and previous employers. It fits the person who is changing careers, has no experience, or whose work history is limited or has gaps. But it may frustrate the reader who wants facts and may create suspicion that it camouflages something.

- Combination: This type is best to use if your background permits. It includes both a chronological and a functional recapitulation of your abilities, skills, and experience.

How to Write Your Résumé

As you prepare your résumé, keep in mind the employers and their needs and tailor each section accordingly.

The following format is frequently recommended. You do not, however, need to follow it slavishly, and you may want to modify it consistent with the aim of hooking the reader quickly. But keep it conservative.

Personal Data. At top and center of the first page, give your name, address, telephone numbers, e-mail address, and fax (optional). Eliminate all references to age, sex, religion, marital status, and health. None of this information can legally be asked for or used by the employer.

Experience. Here you have a choice of chronological, functional, or combination formats. If you use chronological, start with your most recent job experience and work backward. If you use functional, select important skills relevant to the job, such as computer, market research, or managerial, and list your experience under each.

Don't limit your listing to full-time jobs. Include part-time work, internships, volunteer research work, and the like. Your listing should appear thus:

Years Worked/Job Title/Employer/Location/Job Duties and Responsibilities

Education. Don't neglect to include special courses, seminars, and the like. (If your work experience is limited or if you have just finished school, education would probably be listed before experience.) If you are a college graduate or have some college, set up your listing this way:

Institution/ Major/ Grade Point Average
Degree Year/ Location/ Minor (optional)

Skills, Achievements, Honors, Memberships, Activities. Examples of skills are computer software ability, laboratory skills, leadership, and research. Include as achievements and honors any awards you have received: fellowships, scholarships, athletic trophies. Also include here your memberships in professional, community, and academic associations. Be sure to include your activities and any leadership roles in them.

Suggestions and Tips

The résumé is not only appropriate to respond to an ad for a specific job, it can also be sent to companies you have identified as potential employers who may have a need for your skills or for whom you would like to work.

If you are responding to an ad, orient all sections of the résumé to match the employer's needs. Emphasize items that demonstrate your skills and abilities relevant to those needs.

If you are running off a number of résumés and it would be difficult to tailor them to a specific job, include a cover letter when you send them to a possible employer. In this letter, you should refer to those skills, educational assets, and work experiences (as given in the résumé) that would be particularly relevant to the job as indicated in the newspaper ad.

Keep the readability of your résumé foremost in mind. Check it against these criteria:

- No more than two pages. Keep it brief.

- Use 8½-by-11 white or off-white paper.

- Use, or have your professional résumé preparer use, a high-quality preferably laser printer.

- Use a simple typeface. Fonts such as Arial, Times Roman, and Helvetica are appropriate. No more than two typestyles should be used.

- Do not use right-side justified margins.

- Avoid photos, graphics, color.

- Do not use abbreviations.

- Be certain your spelling, grammar, and punctuation are correct. Use a dictionary to ensure accuracy.

- Solicit the aid of others, preferably experienced people, to review your résumé, but use your own judgment about their suggestions.

- Try to learn if your résumé is to be sent to the human resources department or to a specific department head. For the human resources department, your résumé should be straightforward and generic; for a department head you can be more specific and slant your education and background more directly to that department.

The Cover Letter

Your résumé will probably be sent with a cover letter. It should be a brief one, no more than one page. Use it to tell the prospective employer

The English writer George Orwell once took a well-known verse from *Ecclesiastes*:

"I returned, and saw under the sun, that the race is not to the swift, nor the battle to the strong, neither yet bread to the wise, nor yet riches to men of understanding, nor yet favour to men of skill; but time and chance happeneth to them all."

Orwell then translated the verse into the worst sort of business-speak:

"Objective consideration of contemporary phenomena compels the conclusion that success or failure in competitive activities exhibits no tendency to be commensurate with innate capacity, but that a considerable element of the unpredictable must inevitably be taken into account."

that you are interested in the job or the company and are available for an interview. As indicated earlier, use it also to highlight your relevant skills, educational assets, and work experiences, when appropriate.

Be careful about the cover letter. Use simple English and avoid pretentiousness.

Finally, for both your résumé and its cover letter, observe the following rules:

- Tell the truth. The price for getting caught in less than truth or insignificant evasion—a very likely possibility—will damage your reputation, possibly irreparably.

- Present any blemishes on your record in the most favorable way, while still telling the truth.

- If there are blemishes you are unable to clean up, like tax liens, lawsuits, or a criminal history, try for a job in a smaller company, one less likely to conduct an extensive background check.

- Avoid fabricating your educational and job history. These are the most common inventions. When they are exposed, you are likely to be turned down or even lose the job after you are hired.

- Proofread your résumé and the covering letter several times. Have somebody else proofread it also.

The E-Résumé

More and more employers, especially larger companies with computer sophistication and orientation, list available jobs on their Web sites and receive many e-résumés, solicited and unsolicited. It is a pretty fair surmise that the quantity will increase even though most employers still focus on résumés received through traditional sources.

You also should consider using this new avenue to introduce yourself to an employer. To play it safe, you should use both delivery systems—regular-mail résumés and e-mail ones.

Many of the rules for traditional résumé writing apply to e-résumé writing, but some are special. These tips are based on the premise that you have a work history.

Try to ensure that when your résumé is scanned, the essential points are quickly spotted, so it doesn't land on the large pile of rejects. Thus the top of page one contains personal information: name, address, telephone numbers, e-mail address, and fax (optional). Immediately following, list your job objective; be as specific as you can. Follow with your most recent work history, just as on your regular résumé, with years worked, job title, employer, and location, and your job duties and responsibilities. Save page two for education, memberships, and special information like willingness to relocate.

Right up there near the top go your specific skills and knowledge that are relevant to the job, then personal qualities and your accomplishments and achievements. The first half of page one may be especially important because some search engines extract this data to secure hits. Don't be shy about your critical skills that are required in the job. And don't be afraid of redundancy. Do repeat them whenever appropriate in describing your work history.

If possible, use ASCII in your formatting and simple clear fonts, as in your regular résumé, such as Arial and Times Roman. Use no more than two fonts.

AT&T World Net Service adds the following do's and don'ts:

- Don't send an attachment. Most companies discourage attachments because of the possibility that they contain viruses. So even though your résumé might look prettier as an attached Word document, send it in the body of your e-mail. (Save your résumé as a "text only" document, then make any necessary cosmetic changes before you copy and paste it into the e-mail.)

- Don't forget the basics. Just because you may not worry about punctuation and capitalization in your e-mails and instant messages to family and friends doesn't mean you can be equally lax in your résumé.

- Do think about privacy. If you don't want your current employer to see that you're job hunting, be careful where you post your résumé online. Some sites allow you to exclude certain companies from viewing it.

- Do stay up to date. Make notes about where and when you posted your résumé so that you can update it (or remove it) if necessary.

AT&T also suggests some sites that allow you to hunt and post your résumé online:

Monster.com: Nation Job
Head Hunter.net: Flip Dog
America's Job Bank: U.S. Job Bank
Career Builder

However, they caution you to be aware of cost (if any) before posting and to discover whether you will be able to update or delete your résumé at will.

Other Helpful Résumé-Writing Resources

You may be able to find helpful books or pamphlets in your school or local library. Your state employment office (or career center) offers help in résumé writing.

The keywords job résumés in search engines such as Google will turn up many links to Web sites with résumé-writing suggestions and professional résumé-writing organization. Some of those links may also describe how a number of employers are now screening résumés electronically.

Telephone Screening

Sometimes the employer solicits a telephone call from the applicant in place of a résumé. Under some circumstances, this may follow receipt of a résumé. In any case, its purpose is always to screen in candidates who seem to have the necessary qualifications and screen out those who do not.

A telephone screen rarely lasts more than ten minutes. The interviewer may first present a description of the job, and may even highlight its pros and cons, and then ask if the applicant is still interested.

The interviewer is likely to ask questions about the applicant's work history and education and any special requirements that may exist, like willingness to travel or relocate. Based on the answers to these questions, the interviewer will decide whether or not to ask for a résumé, unless he or she already has one, or will ask the applicant to complete the company's application form.

If the interviewer believes the applicant lacks the necessary qualifications, he or she may or may not say so to the applicant.

Interview Screening

A screening interview takes place when the applicant can conveniently visit the employer's office—as, for example, when an applicant drops by and asks to talk to somebody about a job or, perhaps, to pick up an application form. It may take place during a job fair or on a college campus during a recruitment visit. But it is unlikely to take place if, at this early stage, the applicant would have to travel a considerable distance.

A screening interview generally lasts no more than fifteen minutes. It may be quite formal and structured, with the interviewer working from prepared questions.

As with all screening procedures, the content of the interview deals with whether the applicant understands the job and is interested in it and whether he or she possesses the required qualifications.

The Application Form

If you have been through one or more of the screening steps and have been given an application form to fill out and return, it is a pretty good bet that you have been judged to meet the basic qualifications for the job.

Application forms vary a good deal from company to company and from job to job, since special and different requirements may exist.

Unfortunately, you may find the form does not allow you to do justice to your background. And sometimes you may find the forms to be antiquated, since they seem to have a life of their own.

While the content of the application form is not under your control, these factors are:

1. Complete the form in black or dark blue ink (unless told otherwise).
2. Be especially concerned with neatness. Like the résumé, the application form represents you, and you should look at it as a selling document.
3. It may be a good idea, in responding to questions that require a long answer, to write your tentative answer on a separate sheet of paper while experimenting with it and then transfer it to the application form when you are satisfied with it. Be especially careful with your spelling, grammar, and punctuation. It may be a good idea to have

A favorite story from World War II is the one about the GI stationed at some distant base who decided to send weekly flypaper reports to the Pentagon.

He made up his own duplicated form and recorded on it the total fly kill at each mess hall on the base. It was all very official-looking, and the forms were dispatched religiously to Washington every Friday afternoon.

He was a little disappointed that nobody in the army hierarchy reacted, but he doggedly kept counting the dead flies on each roll of flypaper and shooting the results off to the capital.

After a year or so, he was transferred overseas. Within a fortnight, an indignant letter arrived at his old base. Where, the U.S. Army wanted to know, was last week's flypaper report?

someone else proofread it to catch errors you may have missed, before committing the response to the application form.

Especially for Older Workers

- Analyze your résumé and your filled-out application form to make sure you don't appear overqualified. Rename your job titles, so they appear more general and perhaps less imposing.

- Be sure to list new skills, such as computer and technological skills, with some emphasis, as well as courses and development activities you have undertaken, to prove your ability and willingness to keep up to date.

- Consider using a functional format for your résumé. Try to hook the reader by stressing those of your skills that are appropriate to the contemplated position.

Follow the functional portion with a brief but truthful listing of your work history in the chronological portion.

If you leave off, or alter dates, you risk having the reader think you are hiding something.

- Don't list your date of birth, and if your high school and college graduation dates are more than fifteen years old, omit them. Consider whether it might be strategic to omit dates of your jobs also, listing instead the number of years in each.

- One area in which you can practice one-upmanship with younger competitors is in your accomplishments, achievements, knowledge, and experience. Especially point to the promotions you have been given in your previous jobs and the reasons for them. But eliminate from your résumé jobs that go back more than fifteen or so years, unless there is some special reason to include them.

  If lots of time has passed since your last paid employment, perhaps because you have been a volunteer, show how the skills you have used are transferable to the contemplated position.

- In your résumé cover letter, avoid statements in which you give a specific total figure summarizing your work history. "The experience I have gained in my thirty years" should be changed to "I have gained extensive experience." Don't call attention to your age in your cover letter; do call attention to your ability to learn, your flexibility, and your adaptability and stress that your background proves you are dependable, reliable, and stable.

CHAPTER 22

The Depth Interview: Do's and Don'ts and Body Language

Here I lie between two of the best women in the world, my wives. But I requested my relatives to tip me a little toward Tillie.

—*Headstone inscription, Niagara Falls, Canada*

OF ALL THE stages you go through when an employer considers you for a job, this interview is the most important step in hiring and perhaps the one most in your control.

To approach your interview by winging it, by flying by the seat of the pants, is to end up like Harry, the young boy in Louisiana who was always getting into trouble.

One morning, while waiting for the school bus, he pushed the outhouse into the bayou and went off to school as though nothing had happened. When he returned, his father was waiting for him. "Son, did you push the outhouse into the bayou?" "Yes, Father," said Harry. "Like George Washington, I cannot tell a lie."

Harry's father took off his belt. "All right, son, bend over. I'm going to have to whip you." Harry tried to explain that Mr. Washington didn't spank George when he admitted to chopping down the cherry tree. "Yes, son," said Harry's father, "but George's father wasn't in the tree."

The need to pay full attention to details, to be fully prepared, is critical in every step in the hiring process, but it is especially important in preparing for the depth interview.

If you have reached this stage in your job search, it means your resume has been read and not rejected. Perhaps you have had some other brief contact with the prospective employer, such as a phone call or short preliminary interview. Evidently your credentials were promising enough to merit your being asked to complete their application form and return to be interviewed. Be patient while waiting for an appointment. Some companies may not reply for weeks. Continue your search aggressively, even while you wait.

Fundamental Do's and Don'ts

If you are successful at the interview, and assuming your work references and medical examination are OK, you will probably get the job. What, then, does it take to be successful? It takes knowing how to conduct yourself, preparing for the kind of questions you will be asked, being aware of how you and your answers will be evaluated, and being insightful and careful of your interviewer's viewpoint. All these aspects will be discussed in Chapters 22 and 23. Here are the basics. Unless this is your first interview, you will have come across some of them before.

- Don't be late: arrive on time. Short of an earthquake, no excuse will do.

- Make sure you know the interviewer's name and how to pronounce it. If you need to, phone the company to find out. And use Mr. or Ms., not the interviewer's first name.

- Don't forget to bring along an extra copy of your résumé, in case the interviewer has mislaid the one you sent, and bring copies of exhibits or samples of your work also, if this is appropriate. But don't present them unless and until the interviewer asks for them.

- Don't try to be a comedian. No wisecracks. Constantly police your conversation to keep from being verbose or wandering off on tangents.

- Don't ever, at any time in the interview, downgrade or speak ill of a former employer or company, school or teacher. The interviewer is likely to think, We'll probably get the same treatment.

- Don't argue with or debate the interviewer, and don't interrupt. If you'd rather be right, forget about getting the job.

- Don't try to take over the interview or dominate it. Let the interviewer lead the conversation. And make it pleasant rather than stressful or a trial.

- Don't guess, if you don't understand the question. Ask the interviewer for clarification.

- Don't underestimate the interviewer and come up with the answers you think he or she wants. This is not the interviewer's first interview. He or she has heard them all before.

- Don't arrive for the interview with some kind of image of yourself you'll try to role-play. Instead, decide to rise or fall on the basis of who you are.

- There is a chance you may be asked some personal or even illegal questions because the interviewer may very well not be aware of what is legal. Don't blow your stack during the interview. Be prepared in advance on how to answer.

- Finally, don't underplay your abilities and accomplishments. Avoid false modesty. This is not to advocate flamboyance or exaggeration. But a description of the positive aspects of your background and experience, delivered with animation and spirit, is a better approach than, say, Bucky O'Neill's.

It's a sorry frog who won't holler in his own pond.
    —*Lawton Chiles, former governor of Florida*

William "Bucky" O'Neill of Arizona, many years ago, was an unusual politician in that he made candor the focus of his campaigns. Once, when announcing his candidacy for probate judge of Yavapai County, he made the following statement:

"I announce for this office entirely on my own responsibility. There has been no 'anxious public' urging me to do so. There has been no solicitation of friends, nor have the 'wishes of many prominent citizens' made the slightest effort to bluff me into doing it.

"To be frank, it is not a case where the office is wearing itself out hunting the man. Here it is the man wearing himself out for the office, for the simple reason that it is a soft berth with a salary of $2,000 per annum attached.

"While I have no special qualifications—indeed, no advantage over 75 percent of my fellow citizens in the county," Bucky O'Neill went on, "I believe I am fully competent to discharge all the duties incident to the office, if I am elected. If you coincide in this opinion, support me if you see fit. If you do not, you will by no means jeopardize the safety of the universe by defeating me."

Unhappily for O'Neill, his fellow citizens concurred in his assessment and chose someone else.

This list includes a lot of don'ts. Here are some important do's.

- Do stress what you can do for the employer, based on skills you have acquired that you can transfer to the new company. Avoid pleading "I'll do anything."

Emphasize how your knowledge and skills fit the requirements of the job.

• Do follow up the interview with a thank-you note. This not only reinforces a favorable image but also gives you a second chance to remind the interviewer of who you are and of your interest in the position.

Come Prepared

Be informed on as many facets of the company as you can: its size, locations, market, share of market, position within the industry, goals, and mission. This is clear evidence of your interest and also of your initiative. Read Chapter 2, Evaluating a Job, to find the names of directories and governmental sources of information about companies. Public companies publish annual reports. Many companies have their own Web sites. Search engines often list data about companies, as do investment companies. Know the names and titles of the company's officers.

Dress Appropriately

Select attire that suits the industry. An otherwise qualified applicant for a position as a seed sales representative came dressed in a dark conservative suit, white shirt, and dark tie, as though he were applying for a job with IBM or perhaps with a pharmaceutical company.

When Al Horwitz worked in the publicity department of Universal Pictures, one of his clients was the young Shelley Winters. Scheduled to meet a certain Italian producer, she called Horwitz for background information.

"He's a terrible wolf," Horwitz said. "He'll tear the clothes off your back."

"So I'll wear an old dress," said Shelley.

He was turned down. The interviewer felt the farmers and retail seed store owners would regard him as a dude who couldn't understand their business.

Still, in general, the dress code is conservative. Men are best off in a single-breasted suit in a solid dark or conservative color. Women should also be conservatively dressed.

Avoid any item identified with a personal association or belief. Avoid sunglasses; the interviewer will want to be able to see your eyes. Don't overdress.

Your clothes and grooming make an immediate first impression. This is within your control, so make sure the impression is a good one. This helps develop good rapport, early on, with the interviewer.

Body Language

There are a lot of studies about body language. From them it appears that people often regard nonverbal communication as more reliable than what is said verbally. In fact, when people say one thing, but their body language contradicts this and says something else, we tend to believe the body language.

Nonverbal communication during an interview works both ways. It allows the interviewer to focus on your body language to size you up and evaluate what you are saying; it also enables you to focus on the interviewer's body language to judge how you are coming across and make adjustments if they are necessary.

Important Body Parts

Six parts of the body (both yours and the interviewer's) are most important in sending messages.

The Eyes: Even in everyday conversation we refer to eyes, as in *steely-eyed* or *shifty-eyed*. Something that causes surprise or provides unexpected information is referred to as an *eye-opener*.

When two people interact, if both are comfortable in communicating, they generally look each other straight in the eyes. But if you, the applicant, say something that causes discomfort, the interviewer will break off eye contact with you. That's a signal to change your approach, especially because interviewers usually have even more eye contact with you when they listen than when they talk.

The Mouth: At best, a smile lubricates the conversation and helps establish and maintain rapport. But not all smiles are so favorable. Interviewers whose attention wanders away from you will show only a slight upward turn of the lips. They are simply being polite and feigning interest. Have you been too wordy, dull, boring? Better modify what you are saying, so as to connect again.

The Arms: A sign of defensiveness, crossed arms indicates that the interviewer has arrived at a fixed opinion about something. Better not hammer away at the same message; move in another direction.

The Legs: Crossing the legs may also be a sign of defensiveness or disagreement.

The Face: One of the best signals of the interviewer's feelings is his or her facial expression. A poker-faced interviewer doesn't want to give you a clue on where you stand, and there may not be much you can do about it.

The Hands: If the interviewer's finger starts rubbing against shirt or blouse collar, or against neck or head, this often signals frustration or impatience. If the interviewer's finger rubs or strokes the chin or pinches the bridge of the nose, especially with eyes closed or squinting, this signals careful study or appraisal of what you are saying. It is neither agreement nor disagreement; consider whether you ought to continue with more explanation or leave well enough alone.

The interviewer who leans back with both hands clenched in back of the head is in a position of dominance or superiority. When the hands are steepled—the fingertips placed together to form an arch or perhaps a church steeple—you are again dealing with considerable self-confidence, even smugness, even superiority. It may be a good idea to support the feeling; certainly do nothing to antagonize or deflate it.

The interviewer who slowly removes eyeglasses to clean them, or mouths an earpiece, is involved in thought and may be stalling for time or waiting for a chance to ask a question or raise a point. Best to pause and wait for the question or statement.

The interviewer who takes a pair of glasses off and tosses them quickly on the desk may be indicating that he or she is not buying what you are selling. Especially if the interviewer turns away from you, indications are that the interview is over and it is time for you to leave.

Body Clues to Feelings

Attitudes and feelings associated with nonverbal communications, both yours and the interviewer's, can make or break the success of the interview, along with the clues they provide for you.

Uptightness

Clues: Fidgeting, playing with things like pens, watches, keys, coins. Face or lips may be twitching slightly, no eye contact but eyes dart here and there. Laughs at inappropriate times, often clears throat, hand over mouth.

Applicant: Some nervousness on your part is understandable and probably will be excused. But try to control mannerisms because the gestures may distract from the message.

Interviewer: The interviewer may be uptight too, either new to the job or nervously reacting to some other experience. Try to build rapport and emphasize words and actions that reduce the interviewer's stress.

Indifference, Lack of Interest, Impatience

Clues: Eyelids start drooping, head and chin cupped in hand, fingers start drumming, or doodling, foot swings and taps.

Applicant: It's doubtful you'll do this, but if you do, you've struck out.

Interviewer: The interviewer might very well do this; it's a bad sign. Immediately change your approach or topic or body language. Watch out for verbosity or going off onto tangents. Get on with it.

Doubtfulness, Rejection

Clues: No eye contact, body turned slightly away, arms and legs crossed, eyebrows raised, glasses low on nose with eyes peering at you over them. This is not favorable eye contact but is possibly related to poorly fitting glasses or glasses used only for reading.

Applicant: These are not likely to be your gestures.

Interviewer: These are negative signs. You've got some ground to make up. Try to figure out what caused the doubt or rejection. Move away from whatever topic was the cause. Try to change the interviewer's feelings by questions or, in a pinch, probing to find the reasons for the rejection or doubt.

Sincerity

Clues: Person moves closer to the other and leans forward in chair. Hands are open, not clenched. If arms are crossed, they are not tightly so, and are probably resting on thighs. Facial expression is alert but relaxed.

Applicant: If you can assume these gestures, you are signaling that you are comfortable and not nervous. This can help you establish rapport. But don't overdo it.

Interviewer: This is a cooperative attitude. The interviewer wants to meet you halfway. These are favorable signs and represent how the interview ideally should begin. Capitalize on it. Watch closely to make sure interviewer's gestures do not go downhill. If the interview does not begin this way, work further on building rapport.

Assessment, Evaluation

Clues: Hand strokes both cheeks and chin at the same time. Head may be slightly tilted to one side. Body tends to lean forward. Index finger at side of nose. May fuss with glasses or pen to stall for time.

Applicant: These are the perfectly natural gestures of someone who is evaluating what the other person is saying. It signals to the interviewer that you are carefully considering the question before answering it. But don't take too long; you risk letting the interviewer think you are concealing or inventing something.

Interviewer: The interviewer is assessing something you said, against a background that may be favorable or unfavorable. Or the interviewer may be processing in his or her mind where you stand and what question to ask next. Best for you to slow down and give the interviewer a chance to think things through.

Defensiveness

Clues: You can see defensive behavior right away. Arms and legs are crossed tightly. Eye contact is mostly lost. Face is pinched, as are lips. Body is tight, stiff, unyielding. Head is down. Body shifts in chair, away from the other person.

Applicant: You are not likely to assume this posture or these gestures. If you do, recognize that your relationship with the interviewer is in danger of breaking down. You might get into this position if the interviewer has intruded into your private life, perhaps illegally. This is why it is a good idea to prepare how you will react to such a situation in advance of the interview, so you don't lose your cool.

Interviewer: You must say or do something that will change the interviewer's feelings; otherwise the outcome is not likely to be successful. Try to find out what you said or what happened to cause this defensiveness and see if you can backtrack and recover.

Approval, Acceptance, Optimism

Clues: Moves closer to the other person, smiles. Body is straight, erect, but not tense or stiff. Hands and arms are open. Voice is animated, as is facial expression.

Applicant: This is the posture and attitude you should try to project throughout the interview. It tends to promote reciprocity.

Interviewer: The interviewer is conveying a favorable attitude toward you or what you are saying. Try to maintain whatever approach you are using. It is working.

Voice Quality

Another form of nonverbal communications is a change in style or tone of voice. To quote an old cliché, the success of your responses to the questions during the interview depends not only on what you say but how you say it.

The interviewer, consciously or unconsciously, will get a feel for your normal voice tone and style early on; it establishes a kind of benchmark. After that, if your tone and style move from the bench mark, it will be noted and, as with all nonverbal communication, the interviewer will be aware of any situation where your words convey one message and your voice quality another.

Here are some general rules to help you present a successful voice tone and style:

- Try to avoid a monotone. You don't want to interact with a sleepy, bored interviewer, which is what a monotone can produce. Avoid it by varying your volume, rhythm, and pitch (highness or lowness of tone).

- Change the speed of your delivery. When you come to an important point, speak more slowly. Also, pause a couple of seconds to give the interviewer time to process the information you have just provided.

- Present variations in volume. A low volume suggests you are imparting important matters you are sharing with the interviewer, whom you trust. Higher volume suggests animation, energy, enthusiasm.

- Be careful to enunciate clearly and distinctly, and be especially careful not to drop your voice at the end of a sentence, a common failing.

- Try to talk with resonance, but avoid being overly loud.

- Watch the interviewer carefully to see the effect of your voice quality. This is especially important if your voice seems to be lulling the interviewer to sleep.

CHAPTER **23**

The Depth Interview: Content and Evaluation

IN CONDUCTING the interview, the interviewer wants to know, first, can this applicant do the job? In other words, does he or she have the necessary skills? If the answer is yes, is the applicant:

- A reliable person?

- Energetic enough to turn out an acceptable quantity of work?

- Pleasant enough to get along with the boss and the coworkers?

- Committed enough to turn out work of acceptable quality?

- Able to deal with situations that are stressful?

- Reasonably well organized, if the job requires organization?

- Able to make decisions, if the job requires decision making?

You can see that the easiest question is the first one: Does the applicant have the necessary skills? Let's tackle that first.

Evaluating Your Ability

In order to make this kind of evaluation, a company is usually advised to talk to those of their people in a particular job who have proved to be the most productive—the outstanding workers. From these conversations, the company develops a description of the job, along with a list of the most important skills necessary to do it well.

Armed with the job description and skills list, the interviewer knows what to ask the applicant. The aim of the questions is to learn if the candidate possesses these skills and to what degree. The interviewer also already has read the candidate's résumé and completed application, both of which should list work experience and educational background.

These papers and the interview questions developed from the job description are usually enough to enable the interviewer to decide if the candidate has the necessary job skills. For certain jobs, where it is appropriate, the interviewer can ask for samples of the applicant's work or even, for example, ask the applicant to sit down at the computer or whatever other equipment is involved and demonstrate his or her abilities. It is probably fair to say that this is generally the most successful part of the interview, both for the interviewer and for the qualified job candidate.

Evaluating Your Personal Characteristics

The issues that deal with the applicant's personal characteristics are the more difficult.

Is the applicant reasonably well organized if the job requires organization, and able to make decisions if the job requires decision making? Plainly, there is no sense bothering with a particular personal characteristic if it is irrelevant to the job, so many companies make a study of the personal characteristics that *are* relevant. In these well-run companies, interviewers have been trained to ask questions likely to provide answers that contain clues to whether you and the other applicants have the necessary characteristics, or *dimensions,* for the job. These questions are often called *probes.*

When you are interviewed, you may be confronted with questions that probe whether you possess these dimensions. The interviewer will have them in mind, or maybe actually in written form, as questions to be explored and answered.

Here is a list of twelve dimensions, common to many different jobs, that was used in interviewing candidates in an actual company. Not all of them are likely to be used in one of your interviews, only those considered necessary to do the job for which you are applying.

1. Resilience and coping: The ability to deal positively with problems—such as conflict with others or stress-provoking conditions—and to bounce back afterward.
2. Initiative: The ability to take the first step, to originate new ideas or methods, to think and act independently.
3. Commitment to work: Dedication to doing the job or task and to getting results even in the face of difficulty or the need for personal sacrifice.
4. Versatility: The ability to be competent at many things, to be able to turn easily from one job to another, to be adaptable.
5. Impact: The ability to project a favorable first impression.
6. Energy level: The ability to demonstrate high activity at work; the capacity for vigorous action.
7. Planning and organization: The ability to arrange things in an orderly way, to form things into coherent relationships, to devise a system for doing, arranging, or making something; skill in time management.

8. Oral communication skills: The ability to form clear artic-
   ulate statements and to use speech in influencing others.
9. Judgment: The ability to come to opinions about things by
   comparing and deciding, using understanding and good
   sense.
10. Problem solving and decision making: Firmness of mind;
    the ability to make up one's mind, to come to a
    conclusion, to approach a problem with objectivity, to
    base decisions on facts and reason.
11. Sensitivity and empathy: The ability to be aware of outside
    stimuli and impressions and to understand and share
    another's feelings.
12. Persuasiveness: The ability to influence another to take an
    action or adopt a belief by an appeal to reason and/or
    emotion, in a way that the decision seems to come from
    the other person.

It has been said that the real art of conversation is not only to say
the right thing at the right time but also to leave unsaid the wrong
thing at the tempting moment. That's good advice for this section.

The rest of this chapter gives examples of the probes the interviewer is likely to use, discussed under the twelve dimensions just
listed. Again, these are not necessarily the questions you will be
asked, nor do the characteristics being measured necessarily apply to
you. They differ depending on the job. But the probes and dimensions presented here are not unlike those used for a variety of positions. Become familiar with them, and practice how you would
answer. You could even rehearse with another person in the role of
interviewer.

Of course, you will not be asked all the questions listed under
each dimension. The interviewer will choose the ones most likely to
bring forth the most useful answers, based on how the interview
progresses.

The interviewer will then evaluate your responses to these questions and score them according to the guidelines at the bottom of each dimension. The scoring possibilities are minus 2 (the interviewer judges your possession of the dimension to be very poor), minus 1 (poor), 0 (minimally acceptable), plus 1 (good), and plus 2 (excellent).

He or she will then total the scores for all the dimensions and, based on the totals, decide whether you have passed the interview.

Resilience and Coping

1. All of us face rejection from time to time. It might be rejection of an idea we've proposed, permission to do something, or even a turndown in a social situation. Describe a recent situation in which you encountered resistance or rejection. What did you do? How did you feel?
2. What happened the last time you proposed a good idea and it was rejected?
3. How do you deal with rude people? Why?
4. How many times could someone turn you down before you'd give up on them? How would you continue to persist without alienating the individual with whom you were dealing?
5. What is the most significant situation in which you've had to deal with rejection? How did you handle it? How did you feel?
6. What do you feel is the toughest aspect of this job with respect to its emotional aspects? How would you respond? How have you dealt with this in the past?

Scoring Resilience and Coping

−2: Frustrated and unable to perform in the face of rejection or opposition, moody, frequent ups and downs, shows nervous symptoms.

−1: Performance damaged by poor reaction to rejection or opposition, flies off the handle, hotheaded, sarcastic, easily provoked, excitable.

0: Observably vulnerable, but able to handle disappointments and rejections.

+1: Tolerates rejection and remains stable and objective.

+2: Self-motivation and work standards remain high even in the face of frequent disappointments or rejection. Meets turndowns creatively and constructively.

Initiative

1. How do you get your work assignments? Have you ever had the opportunity to generate projects on your own? If yes, can you give me an example of one you've started recently?
2. Describe a situation in which you found your results were not up to company expectation. What did you do to rectify the matter?
3. List the new ideas and suggestions that you have made to your supervisor in the last six months. (The interviewer then picks one to explore in more depth.)
4. Which of your ideas have been accepted by your supervisor? How did you get them adopted?
5. What are your plans for the future? Tell me about what you have done or are doing to make this happen.
6. What have been your most significant accomplishments in school, personal life, and on your last (or present) job?

Scoring Initiative

−2: Lacks any initiative, in a rut, rigid, immobile, wooden.

−1: Passive acceptance of environment. Allows environment to manipulate self. Dislikes situations that have not been structured for him or her. Stereotyped, predetermined.

0: Actively influences events, manipulates environment.

+1: Sometimes takes action beyond what is necessarily called for. Takes constructive action.

+2: Almost always originates action, rather than just responding. Reaches out for ever-increasing responsibility, assumes responsibility for own actions. Innovative, takes imaginative action.

Commitment to Work

1. What personal factors do you consider most important in evaluating yourself or your success?
2. Why did you choose this career?
3. Can you give me examples of experiences on your last (or present) job that you felt were satisfying?
4. In your position, how do you define doing a good job?
5. What do you consider the most important contribution you have made to your organization? Give examples.
6. What have you done in your past work that could have been done better?

Scoring Commitment to Work

−2: Doesn't care whether work is well done; easily distracted from completing job, slipshod.

−1: Only passive interest in whether job is well done. Starts more things than he or she can finish.

0: Adheres to minimum standards called for by job.

+1: Sets somewhat more than minimum standards called for by job. Occasionally works beyond hours required.

+2: Sets high standards, is goal-oriented, disregards time in zest to achieve.

Versatility

1. Going from a small school to a big school must have caused you some transition problems. What were they and how did you cope with them?
2. How was your transition from college to graduate school? Any particular problems?
3. How have you handled conflicting deadlines or tasks in your previous jobs?
4. If you had to relocate to another area of the country, how would you prepare yourself?
5. If you previously had a boss with whom you've disagreed over a major issue, how did you resolve the conflict?

Scoring Versatility

−2: Unable to respond with different approaches or strategies to achieve goal. Inflexible; intolerant "me first" attitude.

−1: Little ability to adjust or cope to reach goals. Blames others; a compromiser when beneficial to self.

0: Adequately adjusts or copes when faced with barriers.

+1: Employs a variety of responses in order to reach goal.

+2: Employs a large variety of responses in order to resolve frustrations and uses different strategies relative to situation.

Impact

(This dimension can be measured from the very beginning of the interview. The following may assist in some circumstances.)

1. What do you believe is the significance of an individual's physical appearance, dress, voice, manner, or eye contact with regard to his or her ability to deal with others?

2. How important do you think an individual's appearance is with respect to being an effective salesperson? Why?
3. When meeting someone for the first time, what makes a good first impression? Why?
4. Many books have been written on first impressions and dressing for success. What's your opinion of the merit of these books and articles?
5. How do *you* make a good first impression?
6. How would you overcome a poor first impression?

Scoring Impact

−2: Creates very poor first impression.

−1: Creates below-average first Impression.

0: Creates neutral first impression.

+1: Creates above-average first impression.

+2: Creates excellent first impression.

Energy Level

1. How do you organize your day?
2. IIow do you catch up on an accumulated backlog of work after a vacation or a conference?
3. What do you do with your spare time?
4. What do you do for exercise?
5. How does your weekend differ from your workweek?
6. What's the best time of day for you to work? The worst? To what do you attribute the difference?

Scoring Energy Level

−2: Very low energy level, lethargic.

−1: Sporadic, works in spurts, looks for easy way out.

0: Chugs along; works steadily and consistently.

+1: Capable of maintaining a high activity level.

+2: Exceptionally high activity level—tireless, a dynamo.

Planning and Organization

1. How do you schedule your time and set priorities?
2. What do you do when your schedule is upset by unforeseen circumstances?
3. Describe how you determine what constitutes top priorities in the performance of your job. Give examples.
4. What are your objectives for this year? Who else knows them? What are you doing to see that they are reached? How are you progressing?
5. How have you organized your responsibilities on your current job? In school?

Scoring Planning and Organization

−2: Unable to establish course of action, or unable to plan proper organization of tasks or appropriate use of resources. Procrastinates unduly.

−1: Barely able to establish course of action, plan, organize, or prioritize.

0: Adequate planning; adequate in establishing goals, budgeting time, prioritizing.

+1: Generally his or her planning of goals for self, time management, and prioritizing are better than average.

+2: Nearly always superior in planning of goals for self. Identifies activities he or she must accomplish to reach goals. Establishes priorities for himself or herself and provides necessary time and resources.

Oral Communication Skills

1. What different approaches do you employ in talking with different types of people? How do you evaluate the effectiveness of these approaches?

2. Have you ever done any public speaking or speaking before groups? Can you give me an example? How did it go? (This factor can be observed from the individual's communications during the interview.)

Scoring Oral Communication Skills

−2: Fails to complete thoughts, uses incorrect grammar, speaks so softly (or loudly) as to interfere with listener's comfort. Rambles, mumbles, no eye contact, no body language to complement words.

−1: Trails off in midsentence, uses awkward grammar, verbose, uses excessive slang or inappropriate vocabulary, speech is slurred, voice inflection inappropriate, uses distracting mannerisms, little eye contact, little body language.

0: Grammar, vocabulary, eye contact, and voice inflection adequate but unremarkable; can express self satisfactorily but without any particular distinction.

+1: Expresses thoughts fully, grammar and sentence structure proper, vocabulary appropriate, complete absence of distracting mannerisms, uses appropriate hand gestures, maintains eye contact.

+2: Expresses thoughts clearly and concisely, enunciates clearly, voice inflection varied, can provide emphasis. Vocabulary, grammar, and sentence structure impressive; body language (eye contact, hand gestures) reinforces impact of words.

Judgment

1. What has been the most difficult decision you've had to make in the past month? Year? Why? What factors did you consider in reaching this decision? How has this decision worked out?
2. Can you give me two examples of good decisions you have made in the last six months? What were the alternatives? Why were your decisions good?

3. What is the biggest decision you have made in the last year? Tell me how you went about it. What alternatives did you consider?
4. In your present (last) job, what decision did you consider the longest before you decided what to do? Tell me about it. Why was it difficult?

Scoring Judgment

−2: Illogical, poor reasons for actions, confused.

−1: Sees no possibility of developing alternative solutions to problems.

0: Logic is mechanical and obvious.

+1: Can develop alternative solutions and reach logical decisions with effort.

+2: Generates an abundance of alternative solutions to problems and evaluates these alternatives objectively.

Problem Solving and Decision Making

1. Have you ever recognized the existence of a problem first, before your boss or others in the organization? Tell me about the actions you took.
2. Why have you decided to leave your current job?
3. What factors did you consider in making decisions in getting your current job? In choosing a college?
4. What was your most difficult decision in the last six months? What made it difficult?
5. What kinds of decisions do you tend to make rapidly and which ones do you take more time on? Give me some examples.
6. Give examples of a situation in which you made up your mind too rapidly. Explain.

Scoring Problem Solving and Decision Making

−2: Cannot identify problems or causes of problems, unable to select relevant information. Not ready to make decisions or render judgments. No commitment or action.

−1: Weak in identifying problems, selects superficial causes. Little commitment, takes minimal action.

0: Identifies problems, causes, and relevant information. Is ready to make decisions and does render judgment but with little commitment or action.

+1: Identifies existing problems as well as those that may arise in future. Well-balanced, practical, direct, and rapid. Ready and willing to make decisions and does so in terms of a commitment to action.

+2: Identifies problems accurately and easily, has the ability to gather facts to make a decision. Analysis is thorough and penetrating. Makes decisions that are firm, direct, timely. Unaffected by opportunism or unpopularity of decision. Once decision is made, becomes fairly committed.

Sensitivity and Empathy

1. What specific problem has your supervisor brought to you recently? How did you handle it?
2. Have you perceived any problem you have caused others? How are you going to avoid doing it again?
3. How do you go about collecting personal information regarding your customers' likes and dislikes?
4. When selling an account, how do you determine when you are pushing too hard? How do you determine when you should back off?

5. Recall a time when someone was aggressive toward you. How did you feel about that person at that moment? How do you think they felt toward you? How did you respond?
6. Recall a time when someone ignored you. How did you feel about that person at that moment? How do you think they felt toward you? How did you respond?

Scoring Sensitivity and Empathy

−2: Creates hostility or defensiveness; is personally involved, overly sensitive, prejudiced.

−1: Indifferent to people; theoretical in manner or tries, through force, to influence people. Unduly direct and blunt.

0: Adequate, logical, mechanical, minimal warmth.

+1: Tries to remove barrier. Understanding and empathic, genuine feelings and consideration for others.

+2: Mutual exploration and respect, mutual reciprocity. Sensitive to others, a good listener.

Persuasiveness

1. What was the best idea you tried to sell to your supervisor that was not accepted? Why wasn't it, and what did you do?
2. Tell me about your toughest experience in dealing with a person and how you handled it.
3. Have you ever taken a training course? What? When? Where was it of most value? Least value?
4. Recall a time when someone disagreed with you and you changed their point of view. Describe in detail how you went about doing it.
5. Recall a time when someone couldn't arrive at a decision. Describe in detail how you helped them "get off the fence."

Scoring Persuasiveness

−2: Unable to organize or present material in a convincing manner to gain agreement or acceptance.

−1: Poorly organized; uses irrelevant material to gain agreement.

0: Organized and moderately convincing and persuasive.

+1: Organized and generally convincing and persuasive.

+2: Uses data and arguments in a manner that will motivate others to make a decision.

CHAPTER **24**

The Hiring Process: Final Steps

IF YOU HAVE impressed the interviewer favorably, you can anticipate that a few last checks will be made, but they are basically not in your control. All these steps take place in the latter stages of the hiring process, because outside people are involved and because some of the procedures are expensive.

Work References

Most companies check work references. They do so by phone, preferring to get information from the applicant's past supervisors rather than from the previous human resources or personnel departments. There are two reasons for the check: To verify factual information, like dates of employment, job title, duties, and responsibilities, and to obtain information about the applicant's work habits, industriousness, and the like.

Either the interviewer or the prospective supervisor is usually the person who does the check. He or she may follow up leads that arose from the interview or another step in the hiring procedure, about which more information is desired, or even follow up hunches.

Employers regard a check with the applicant's most recent employer as most valuable, on the basis that recent work habits and behavior can provide the best clues to future behavior.

Other Background Checks

Years ago, applicants were asked to supply the names of personal references, who usually turned out to be physicians, clergymen, and other contacts who could not supply information about the applicant's work habits but almost invariably provided favorable references. Most companies no longer bother.

When educational background is checked, it is usually simply to confirm dates of attendance, degree or diploma, and other facts.

Some companies additionally perform credit checks, but to do so they must obtain permission from the applicant and must agree to provide the applicant with the report.

Medical Examination

The company may include a medical examination as part of the hiring policy. The purpose is to establish the presence or absence of preexisting conditions that need to be identified, to avoid their becoming the responsibilities of the employer later.

Usually the company has the examination performed by its own medical department or by designated physicians.

Selection Tests

Some companies ask the applicant to take selection tests. These tests are also subject to civil rights legislation and must measure dimensions and personal characteristics directly related to the position.

Sherlock Holmes and Dr. Watson go camping. They pitch their tent under the stars and fall sleep. Sometime in the middle of the night, Holmes wakes Watson up. "Watson, look up at the sky and tell me what you deduce."

Watson says, "I see millions of stars, and even if only a few of them have planets, it's quite likely there are some planets like Earth, and if there are a few planets like Earth out there, there might also be life."

Holmes replies, "Watson, you idiot, somebody stole our tent!"

Since the number and kinds of tests vary greatly, depending on the job and the company, there is no point in describing them further.

The Final Exam

Four Duke University sophomores taking organic chemistry were doing so well on all the quizzes, midterms and labs that each had an A so far for the semester. Confident of success, the four friends decided to party at the University of Virginia on the weekend before finals.

They had a great time. But after all the hearty partying, they slept all day Sunday and didn't make it back to Duke until early Monday morning.

Rather than take the final exam, they went to their professor *after* the final and explained that they had gone to UVA for the weekend, had a flat on the way back, didn't have a spare, couldn't get help for a long time, and as a result, they missed the final.

The professor thought it over and then agreed they take a makeup exam the following day. Elated and relieved, the guys studied that night and went in at the time the professor had told them. He placed them in separate rooms, handed each of them a test booklet, and told them to begin. They looked at the first question, worth 5 points. It was something simple about free radical formation. Cool, they thought. One even said to himself, in his separate room, "This is going to be easy."

Each finished the problem and turned the page. On the second page was written: For 95 points, *which tire?*

CHAPTER 25

Jobs for Older Workers

Age is a question of mind over matter. If you don't mind,
it don't matter.

—*Satchel Paige*

ISN'T GETTING A job the same for older workers as for young ones?
Why is a separate chapter necessary?

It's true that many of the challenges, problems, and obstacles to
be overcome by older workers are the same. But some are different,
so different strategies and tactics need to be employed.

This chapter contains general information to help older workers
in finding and getting jobs or, if desired, in changing careers. Job
search strategies and tactics for writing résumés especially appropriate for older workers were given in Chapters 20 and 21, and
promising fields for older workers to consider were listed at the end
of Chapter 5.

The Age Range of Older Workers

If you searched the Internet for information about older workers and jobs, you might be surprised to find that people fifty and older are described as older workers or seniors. Some Web sites even offer advice for older workers of forty! There's even a word—quadragenerian—for someone who is between forty and fifty years of age.

According to a Cornell University study, 90 percent of retirees still work—to keep active and productive and for social interaction. Money is seldom their main motivator. They are observing the old adage, "When you rest, you rust," a philosophy that has the support of the medical community.

The fastest-growing age group in the workforce is between fifty-five and sixty-four. Eighty percent of these baby boomers expect to work during their retirement years, says the Employee Benefit Research Institute of the American Savings Education Council. A study by the AARP yielded similar results.

The baby boomers' reasons for working were as follows:

- Enjoy working   35%

- Need extra income   23%

- Want to start a business   17%

- Want to try something different   5%

In the year 2000, almost 13 percent of the labor force consisted of people age sixty-five and older, according to the U.S. Bureau of Labor Statistics. This figure was up from 10.8 percent in 1985. From 2000 to 2006, the U.S. Census Bureau reports, the over-fifty population will jump 50 percent.

Stereotypes of Older Workers

Stereotypes—oversimplified and often prejudiced judgments—enable us to classify people quickly and easily, whether or not there is any supporting evidence.

Not surprisingly, older workers are often the victims of stereo-typing, unfair as this usually is. Be prepared to encounter them in your search for a job or in your career shift.

Here is a list of some of the most common but inaccurate opinions about older workers.

- They get sick more often, are absent more often, and therefore cost more than younger workers.

- They exhibit greater job turnover.

- They learn new skills slowly, if they learn them at all.

- They tend to be inflexible ("We didn't do it that way at my last job").

- They cost more because, through seniority, they are entitled to longer vacations and larger pensions.

Your job is to counter these stereotypes with the following realities, using your most persuasive skills:

- A number of studies indicate that older workers lose fewer days because of absenteeism or illness than younger workers.

- The U.S. Bureau of Labor Statistics, reporting on 1998 figures, noted that workers ages forty-five to fifty-four stayed on the job twice as long as those ages twenty-five to thirty-four.

- Proof of the learning ability of workers fifty and over is the fact that they are the fastest-growing group of computer and Internet users. Community colleges, universities, high schools, and technical schools have greatly expanded the courses they offer, to accommodate the demands of older workers who want to acquire these new skills.

- The cost of "longer vacations" and "larger salaries and pensions," which are morale boosters for younger workers, is outweighed by the lower turnover rate of older workers. Turnover is expensive for a company in terms of recruiting and training.

You can also stress any recent accomplishment that shows your flexibility and ability to adapt to changes and new needs. Point out that age is not connected to one's ability to learn new skills or new ways of doing things. Focus on your willingness to handle short-term assignments others may be unable or unwilling to take on. Point out that you don't require the salary and benefits needed by younger workers.

It is well known to physicians and scientists that some people, at sixty, look, act, and function like fifty-year-olds or less and that others at fifty look and act fifteen years older. Make sure you dress in fashionable good taste and act with animation and enthusiasm.

Older workers approach their jobs with the mature judgment that younger workers often lack; they can act as role models and mentors. They are likely to analyze new procedures based on past experience, reject the unrealistic, and accept those new approaches that are sound. They have an understanding of business unmatched by their juniors. And they have proved more dependable and better able to solve problems.

More facts and figures about older workers can be secured online (www.maturityworks.org/news/stats.html).

Are You Considering a Career Shift?

This book's Introduction presented a list of problems and uncertainties that may exist in the minds of today's workers. Many of them especially related to older workers are addressed throughout the book. If you are rethinking your career and considering a career shift, you should be very cautious about making a change in an economically uncertain employment climate. Yet it is tempting to succumb to such enticements. When you are down-in-the-mouth about your job, alternatives look more attractive than they really are.

Most experts say it is advisable to have a job lined up, even if it is only a temporary one, before you say good-bye to your present employer. Or, as a last resort, if you feel you must quit, have at least a year's worth of living expenses as a backup.

Most important, line up a "committee" of family members, informed friends, and people familiar with the industry you're in or considering going into. Use them as a sounding board, so your career moves are not impetuous but based on careful analysis.

Tactics and Strategies

If you suspect you have been discriminated against because of your age, contact the Equal Employment Opportunity Commission (EEOC), in person, by mail, or on the Internet (www.eeoc.com). The federal Age Discrimination in Employment Act (ADEA) forbids employers to fire, refuse to hire, or otherwise discriminate against anyone forty years of age and older. Proving age discrimination can be difficult and expensive, but if you consider it worthwhile, consult an employment attorney. (Find one in your state through the National Employment Lawyers Association.)

If you are considering changing jobs, closely examine the benefits available to you in the new job. Compare your possible new employer's benefit package with your present one. Study the advantages and disadvantages of rolling your present retirement plan into the prospective new one, or perhaps into your own IRA. Health care insurance can be rolled over, but compare the old plan with the new one. Is the life and disability insurance program equal or superior to the old?

Certain factors can make the search for a new job take longer (nearly twice as long, says one study) for older workers than for younger ones. Choosing to switch careers or electing to find a new job with more money or a higher title are some of the factors.

Make sure your skills are up to date, whatever your area of experience. A great many jobs today require computer skills, such as word processing, database, spreadsheet, power-point, and other presentation applications as well as the ability to use the Internet. If necessary, enroll in courses, usually available in high schools, community colleges, and universities.

Important as networking is for all job seekers, it is even more important for older people. Because of your experience, you are likely to have more contacts than younger competitors. Unlike entry-level jobs, jobs for older workers are less likely to be advertised. Find out about them by networking.

Don't decide to take a month off before you start your search. Such a gap between jobs doesn't look good and can make landing a job harder.

Consider innovative and unconventional relationships offered by some companies. Such relationships include compressed workweeks, flextime, part-time work, job sharing, and telecommuting. These and other arrangements can be negotiated between you and the employer. They may be especially attractive and practical if you are receiving health benefits and a pension from a previous employer and being active and productive means as much to you as an income.

Certain companies have programs for retirees who are willing to work a limited number of hours a year. Companies with these programs include Avaya, PepsiCo, Lockheed Martin, and certain divisions of IBM and GE.

Sometimes jobs are available at odd hours when younger workers, with family obligations, are unable or unwilling to work.

Opportunities sometimes come up for working as a consultant during a hiring freeze or for a temporary job while a military reservist is on active duty.

Organizations That Welcome Older Workers

A growing number of companies are making serious and conscious efforts to attract older job seekers. Some of them offer full-time jobs. Others, like McDonald's, offer flexible part-time jobs with benefits.

Days Inn says older workers have a stabilizing influence on younger workers and are accustomed to changes in the way a business operates.

Motorola Corporation, in inviting applications from mature job seekers, feels much the same way and refers to their superior understanding of business.

Oracle and GTE offer technology training programs.

CVS, the major drugstore chain, is readying itself to attract baby boomers who plan to work in retirement. In fact, workers age fifty and older now constitute 14 percent of the CVS workforce, up from 7 percent ten years ago. They explain that older workers are dependable and responsible, demonstrate a caring attitude toward customers, and set good examples for junior workers.

The AARP annually lists its "Best Companies for Workers Over 50," among which currently are ABN AMRO North America, Avis Rent-A-Car System, Foley's Department Stores, Hyatt Hotels and Resorts, and Prudential Insurance Company of America. Locate them online (www.aarp.org/bestcompanies).

Teaching is an important area to consider. The Department of Education estimated in 1999 that more than 2 million new teachers will be needed in the next ten years to replace retiring baby boomers and to answer the educational needs of a growing number of children. The downside of teaching is the low pay, starting at $28,000 a year on average and reaching a high of $42,000 after several years. A bachelor's degree is needed, although a temporary job may be secured until the necessary credentials are acquired.

The upside includes summers off and the good benefits that are usually offered. If your interests and values are appropriate, the experience of teaching youngsters can be rewarding.

Private and Government-Funded Services

The Service Corps of Retired Executives (SCORE) is one of the oldest resources for new entrepreneurs. Its retired-executive volunteers function as advisers, helping people of any age on all subjects relevant to operating a business, including how and where to get funding.

The AARP (formerly the American Association for Retired Persons) provides seminars on such subjects as résumé writing, networking, new opportunities, reentering the workforce, and career planning after retirement. Contact them at (800) 424-3410 (or http://www.aarp.com) to find seminars near you. Look for career seminars for AARP members offered through Drake Beam Morin.

A service to be found on the Web specializes in locating jobs for older people, welfare recipients, dislocated workers, and others who are looking for work and need income (www.ExperienceWorks.org).

For career counseling try: Five O'Clock Club, 300 East 40th Street, #6C, New York, NY 10016; phone (212) 286-4500.

Executives and senior professionals whose compensation level is $100,000 and above are eligible to join ExecuNet, an organization that helps in career networking and providing career management information. Contact ExecuNet, Inc., 25 Van Zant Street, Norwalk, CT 06855; phone (800) 637-3126; fax (203) 851-5177; Web address: http//www.execunet.com or e-mail: execunet@exe cunet.com

Forty Plus, a similar organization, also provides career networking opportunities, job search programs, and other resources, for managers, executives, and professionals who earn more than $40,000. Access their California Web site and click on local chapters nationally (http://www/fortyplus.org).

A service for older workers managed by the National Council on the Aging provides resources to help job seekers find work (www.ncoa.org).

One Web site allows you to post your résumé and a summary of your skills for full-time, part-time, temporary, occasional, and flexible jobs (www.SeniorJobBank.org).

The Employment and Training Administration of the U.S. Department of Labor provides a part-time employment program for low-income individuals who are age fifty-five or over and are paid the federal or state minimum wage, whichever is higher.

Contact Senior Community Service Employment Program, or SCSEP (http://wdsc.doleta.gov/seniors). SCSEP also funds programs for job training and work skills for seniors.

If you are fifty-five or older and are looking to upgrade your skills, a program that offers training and employment, using community service, currently operates in the District of Columbia and twenty-seven states. They also maintain job clubs to assist in networking, résumé preparation, and training in behaviors. The service is free (http://wdsc.doleta.gov/seniors).

Volunteer Work

Many older workers are volunteers. These people have become restless in retirement and need more challenging ways to occupy their time. They find that staying mentally and physically active keeps them younger. As a result, volunteering becomes especially attractive.

There are, of course, many opportunities: in nonprofit organizations, professional organizations, government-sponsored agencies, and university-run programs. But it is important to select activities that are in harmony with your personal qualities. Do political issues turn you on? Does socialization, especially with members of your own profession or field of work, motivate you?

The exercises in Part III that give you insights into your values, personality, interests, and job performance can also provide you with answers to questions you may have on where to start as a volunteer.

The Retired and Senior Volunteer Program (RSVP) of the National Service Corps has 1,300 nationwide programs into which they try to place people based on interests and experience. The Service Corps of Retired Executives (SCORE) mentioned earlier, enrolls volunteers to act as mentors and counselors to entrepreneurs. Watch local newspapers and magazines for community programs that welcome volunteers for a variety of other activities.

Keep in mind that every age has its advantages and your mature years have their compensations. Samuel Johnson said, "As a man advances in life, he gets what is better than admiration—judgment, to estimate things at their true value." And the homespun philosopher

Finley Peter Dunne, in "Old Age," commented, "Many a man that couldn't direct ye to the drugstore on th' corner when he was thirty will get a respectful hearin' when age has further impaired his mind."

And, to reinforce your confidence in your ability to learn new things, think of what author W. Somerset Maugham said: "When I was young I was amazed at Plutarch's statement that the elder Cato began at the age of eighty to learn Greek. I am amazed no longer. Old age is ready to undertake tasks that youth shirked because they would take too long."

EPILOGUE

THERE ARE THREE decisions I hope you will have arrived at by the end of this book. Two of these are resolutions on what not to do; the other is a positive way of thinking.

1. If you have lost your job and have embarked on the difficult process of finding work or if you are employed but unhappy with your job, you must recognize that it does no good to berate the fates and whine about your condition. Walt Whitman, in "Animals" in his collection of poems *Song of Myself* has this lesson:

    I think I would turn and live with animals, they are so placid
        and self-contained,
    I stand and look at them long and long.
    They do not sweat and whine about their condition;
    They do not lie awake in the dark and weep for their sins;
    They do not make me sick discussing their duty to God;
    Not one is dissatisfied—not one is demented with the mania
        of owning things;

273

Not one kneels to another, nor to his kind that lived thousands of years ago;
Not one is respectable or industrious over the whole earth.

Finding a job that is a good fit requires analysis, activity, and a
positive mental attitude, just like every other mature challenge.

2. Starting a new career does not mean hopping from job to
   job, like Rudyard Kipling's cockney in his poem "Sestina
   of the Tramp-Royal," hoping that a kind of providence
   will guide you into the right one:

   But, Gawd, what things are they I 'aven't done?
   I've turned my 'and to most an' turned it good,
   In various situations round the world—
   For 'im that doth not work must surely die;
   But that's no reason man should labour all
   'Is life on one same shift—life's none so long.

3. But it does mean that if you have studied who you are,
   what's out there, and what's the fit, and if the timing is
   right for you and your family, that you will exert the
   energy and the courage to act on your analysis, as did
   Robert Frost in "The Road Not Taken":

   Two roads diverged in a yellow wood,
   And sorry I could not travel both
   And be the one traveler, long I stood
   And looked down one as far as I could
   To where it bent in the undergrowth;
   I shall be telling this with a sigh
   Somewhere ages and ages hence:
   Two roads diverged in a wood, and I—
   I took the one less traveled by,
   And that has made all the difference.